FAITH
THE ESSENCE
OF TRUE RELIGION

FAITH
THE ESSENCE
OF TRUE RELIGION

GORDON B. HINCKLEY

Deseret Book Company
Salt Lake City, Utah

This book is not an official publication of The Church of Jesus Christ of Latter-day Saints. It has been prepared by the author, and he alone is responsible for the contents.

Library of Congress Cataloging-in-Publication Data

Hinckley, Gordon Bitner, 1910–
    Faith : the essence of true religion / by Gordon B. Hinckley.
      p. cm.
    ISBN 0-87579-270-7
    1. Spiritual life—Mormon authors. 2. Faith. 3. Mormon Church—
Doctrines. 4. Church of Jesus Christ of Latter-day Saints—
Doctrines. I. Title.
BX8656.H55 1989
234'.2—dc20   89-37642
                                 CIP

Printed in the United States of America

10   9   8   7   6   5   4   3   2   1

CONTENTS

CHAPTER 1

FAITH, THE ESSENCE OF TRUE RELIGION

Some time ago a prominent journalist from a national publication spoke in Salt Lake City. I did not hear him, but I read the newspaper reports of his remarks. He is quoted as having said, "Certitude is the enemy of religion." The words attributed to him have stirred within me much reflection. Certitude, which I define as complete and total assurance, is not the enemy of religion. It is of its very essence.

Certitude is certainty. It is conviction. It is the power of faith that approaches knowledge — yes, that even becomes knowledge. It evokes enthusiasm, and there is no asset comparable to enthusiasm in overcoming opposition, prejudice, and indifference. Great buildings were never constructed on uncertain foundations. Great causes were never brought to success by vacillating leaders. The gospel was never expounded to the convincing of others without certainty. Faith, which is of the very essence of personal conviction, has always been and always must be at the root of religious practice and endeavor.

There was no uncertainty in Peter's mind when the Lord asked him, "Whom say ye that I am? And Simon Peter answered and said, Thou art the Christ, the Son of the living God." (Matthew 16:15-16.)

Nor was there any doubt on the part of Peter when the

1

Lord taught the multitude in Capernaum, declaring himself to be the bread of life. Many of his disciples, who would not accept his teaching, "went back, and walked no more with him. Then said Jesus unto the twelve, Will ye also go away? Then Simon Peter answered him, Lord, to whom shall we go? thou hast the words of eternal life. And we believe and are sure that thou art that Christ, the Son of the living God." (John 6:66-69.)

Following the death of the Savior, would his apostles have carried on, teaching his doctrine, even giving their lives in the most painful of circumstances, if there were any uncertainty concerning him whom they represented and whose doctrine they taught? There was no lack of certitude on the part of Paul after he had seen a light and heard a voice while en route to Damascus to persecute the Christians. For more than three decades after that, he devoted his time, his strength, his life to the spreading of the gospel of the resurrected Lord. Without regard for personal comfort or safety, he traveled over the known world of his time, declaring that "neither death, nor life, nor angels, nor principalities, nor powers, nor things present, nor things to come, nor height, nor depth, nor any other creature, shall be able to separate us from the love of God, which is in Christ Jesus our Lord." (Romans 8:38-39.)

Executed in Rome, Paul sealed with his death his final testimony of his conviction of the divine sonship of Jesus Christ. So it was with the early Christians, thousands upon thousands of them, who suffered imprisonment, torture, and death rather than recant their stated beliefs in the life and resurrection of the Son of God. Would there ever have been a Reformation without the certitude that drove with boldness such giants as Luther, Hess, Zwingli, and others of their kind?

As it was anciently, so has it been in modern times. Without certitude on the part of believers, a religious cause becomes soft, without muscle, without the driving force that would broaden its influence and capture the hearts and affections of men and women. Theology may be argued over, but personal testimony, coupled with performance, cannot be refuted. This gospel dispensation, of which we are the beneficiaries, opened with a glorious vision in which the Father and the Son appeared to the boy Joseph Smith. Having had that experience, the boy recounted it to one of the preachers of the community, who treated the account "with great contempt, saying it was all of the devil, that there were no such things as visions or revelations in these days." (Joseph Smith–History 1:21.)

Others took up the cry against him. He became the object of severe persecution. But, he said, "I had actually seen a light, and in the midst of that light I saw two Personages, and they did in reality speak to me; and though I was hated and persecuted for saying that I had seen a vision, yet it was true; and while they were persecuting me, reviling me, and speaking all manner of evil against me falsely for so saying, I was led to say in my heart: Why persecute me for telling the truth? I have actually seen a vision; and who am I that I can withstand God, or why does the world think to make me deny what I have actually seen? For I had seen a vision; I knew it , and I knew that God knew it, and I could not deny it, neither dared I do it." (JS–H 1:25.)

There is no lack of certitude in that statement. For Joseph Smith, that experience was as real as the warmth of the sun at noonday. He never flagged nor wavered in his conviction. Listen to his later testimony of the risen Lord:

"And now, after the many testimonies which have been given of him, this is the testimony, last of all, which we give of him: That he lives! For we saw him, even on the right hand of God; and we heard the voice bearing record that he is the Only Begotten of the Father—that by him, and through him, and of him, the worlds are and were created, and the inhabitants thereof are begotten sons and daughters unto God." (D&C 76:22-24.)

So certain was he of the cause he led, so sure of his divinely given calling, that he placed them above the value of his own life. With prescient knowledge of his forthcoming death, he surrendered himself to those who would deliver him defenseless into the hands of a mob. He sealed his testimony with his life's blood.

It was so with his followers. One will find no evidence, not a scintilla of it, that certitude was the enemy of religion in their lives and actions. Time after time they left their comfortable homes, first in New York, then in Ohio and Missouri, later in Illinois; and even after reaching the Salt Lake Valley many left again to plant colonies over a vast area of the West. Why? Because of their faith in the cause of which they were a part.

Many died in those long and difficult journeys, the victims of disease, exposure to the elements, and the brutal attacks of their enemies. Some six thousand lie buried somewhere between the Missouri River and the Salt Lake Valley. Their love for the truth meant more to them than did life itself.

It has been thus ever since. I recorded these beautiful words as President David O. McKay spoke them to a small group some years ago: "As absolute as the certainty that you have in your hearts that tonight will be followed by dawn tomorrow morning, so is my assurance that Jesus Christ is the Savior of mankind, the light that will dispel the darkness of the world, through the gospel restored by direct revelation to the Prophet Joseph Smith."

Our beloved President Spencer W. Kimball said: "I know that Jesus Christ is the Son of the living God and that he was crucified for the sins of the world. He is my friend, my Savior, my Lord, my God." (*Ensign,* November 1978, p. 73.)

It is that kind of certitude that has moved The Church of Jesus Christ of Latter-day Saints forward in the face of persecution, ridicule, sacrifice of fortune, the leaving of loved ones to travel to distant lands to carry the gospel message. That conviction motivates today as it has done from the beginning of this work. Faith in the hearts of millions that this cause is true, that God is our Eternal Father, and that Jesus is the Christ must ever be the great motivating force in our lives.

We have approximately forty thousand missionaries in the field, at a cost of millions of dollars to their families. Why do they do it? Because of their conviction of the truth of this work. The membership of the Church is now approaching seven million. What is the reason for this phenomenal growth? It is because certainty comes into the hearts of hundreds of thousands of converts each year, converts who are touched by the power of the Holy Ghost. We have a great functioning and effective welfare program. Those who view it marvel at it. It works only because of the faith of those who participate in it.

With the growth of the Church we must build new houses of worship, many hundreds of them. They are costly. But the people give of their means, not only for this purpose, but in the regular and faithful payment of their tithes, because of the certitude of the truth of this work.

The marvelous and wonderful thing is that any individual who desires to know the truth may receive that conviction. The Lord himself gave the formula when he said, "If any man will do [God's]will, he shall know of the doctrine, whether it be of God, or whether I speak of myself." (John 7:17.)

It will take study of the word of God. It will take prayer and anxious seeking of the source of all truth. It will take living the gospel, an experiment, if you please, in following the teachings. I do not hesitate to promise, because I know from personal experience, that out of all of this will come, by the power of the Holy Ghost, a conviction, a testimony, a certain knowledge.

Many people in the world seem unable to believe that. What they do not realize is that the things of God are understood only by the Spirit of God. There must be effort. There must be humility. There must be prayer. But the results are certain and the testimony is sure.

If the Latter-day Saints, as individuals, ever lose that certitude, the Church will dwindle as so many other churches have. But I have no fear of that. I am confident that an ever-

5

enlarging membership will seek for and find that personal conviction which we call testimony, which comes by the power of the Holy Ghost, and which can weather the storms of adversity.

To those who vacillate, who equivocate, who qualify their assertions with uncertainty when speaking of the things of God, these words from the book of Revelation are appropriate: "I know thy works, that thou art neither cold nor hot: I would thou wert cold or hot. So then because thou art lukewarm, and neither cold nor hot, I will spue thee out of my mouth." (Revelation 3:15-16.)

With certitude I give you my witness of the truth. I know that God our Eternal Father lives. I know that Jesus is the Christ, the Savior and Redeemer of mankind, the author of our salvation. I know that this work of which we are a part is the work of God; that this is the Church of Jesus Christ. Great is our opportunity for service therein and strong and certain is our faith concerning it.

CHAPTER 2

THE CORNERSTONES OF OUR FAITH

When the Church builds a new temple, a cornerstone ceremony is held in harmony with a tradition that goes back to ancient times. Before the general use of concrete, the foundation walls of the building were laid with large stones. A trench would be dug, and stones would be placed as footings. Starting at a point of beginning, the foundation wall would be run in one direction to a cornerstone; then the corner would be turned and the wall run to the next corner, where another stone was placed, from which the wall would be run to the next corner, and from there to the point of beginning.

In many instances, including the construction of early temples in the Church, cornerstones were used at each junction point of the walls and put in place with ceremony. The final stone was spoken of as the chief cornerstone, and its placement became the reason for much celebration. With this cornerstone in position, the foundation was ready for the superstructure. Hence the analogy that Paul used in describing the true church: "Now therefore ye are no more strangers and foreigners, but fellowcitizens with the saints, and of the household of God; and are built upon the foundation of the apostles and prophets, Jesus Christ himself being the chief corner stone; in whom all the building fitly framed together groweth unto an holy temple in the Lord." (Ephesians 2:19-21.)

7

We have basic cornerstones on which the latter-day church has been established by the Lord and built, "fitly framed together." They are absolutely fundamental to this work, the very foundation, anchors on which it stands. The first, or chief, cornerstone we recognize and honor as the Lord Jesus Christ. The second is the vision given the Prophet Joseph Smith when the Father and the Son appeared to him. The third is the Book of Mormon, which speaks as a voice from the dust with the words of ancient prophets declaring the divinity and reality of the Savior of mankind. The fourth is the priesthood with all of its powers and authority, whereby men act in the name of God in administering the affairs of his kingdom. May I comment on each of these.

Absolutely basic to our faith is our testimony of Jesus Christ as the Son of God, who under a divine plan was born in Bethlehem of Judea. He grew in Nazareth as the carpenter's son, carrying within him the elements of both mortality and immortality received, respectively, from his earthly mother and his Heavenly Father.

In the course of his brief earthly ministry, Jesus walked the dusty roads of Palestine, healing the sick, causing the blind to see, raising the dead, teaching doctrines both transcendent and beautiful. He was, as Isaiah had prophesied, "a man of sorrows, and acquainted with grief." (Isaiah 53:3.) He reached out to those whose burdens were heavy and invited them to cast their burdens upon him, declaring, "My yoke is easy, and my burden is light." (Matthew 11:30.) He "went about doing good," and was hated for it. (Acts 10:38.) His enemies went against him. He was seized, tried on spurious charges, convicted to satisfy the cries of the mob, and condemned to die on Calvary's cross. The nails pierced his hands and feet, and he hung in agony and pain, giving himself a ransom for the sins of all men. He died crying out, "Father, forgive them; for they know not what they do." (Luke 23:34.)

Jesus was buried in a borrowed tomb, and on the third day he rose from the grave. He came forth triumphant, in a victory over death, the firstfruits of all that slept. With his resurrection came the promise to all mankind that life is everlasting, that even as in Adam all die, in Christ all are made alive. (See 1 Corinthians 15:20-22.) Nothing in all of human history equals the wonder, the splendor, the magnitude, or the fruits of the matchless life of the Son of God, who died for each of us. He is our Savior. He is our Redeemer. As Isaiah foretold, "His name shall be called Wonderful, Counsellor, The mighty God, The everlasting Father, The Prince of Peace." (Isaiah 9:6.)

He is the chief cornerstone of the church which bears his name, The Church of Jesus Christ of Latter-day Saints. There is no other name given among men whereby we can be saved. (See Acts 4:12.) He is the author of our salvation, the giver of eternal life. (See Hebrews 5:9.) There is none to equal him. There never has been. There never will be. Thanks be to God for the gift of his Beloved Son, who gave his life that we might live, and who is the chief, immovable cornerstone of our faith and his church.

The second cornerstone is the first vision of the Prophet Joseph Smith. The year was 1820; the season, spring. The boy with questions walked into a grove on his father's farm. There, finding himself alone, he pleaded in prayer for that wisdom which James promised would be given liberally to those who ask of God in faith. (See James 1:5.) There, in circumstances that he has described in much detail, he beheld the Father and the Son, the great God of the universe and the risen Lord, both of whom spoke to him.

This transcendent experience opened the marvelous work of restoration. It lifted the curtain on the long-promised "dispensation of the fulness of times."

For more than a century and a half, enemies, critics, and some would-be scholars have worn out their lives trying to disprove the validity of that vision. Of course they cannot understand it. The things of God are understood by the Spirit of God. There had been nothing of comparable magnitude since the Son of God walked the earth in mortality. Without it as a foundation stone for our faith and organization, we have nothing. With it, we have everything.

Much has been written, much will be written, in an effort to explain it away. The finite mind cannot comprehend it. But the testimony of the Holy Spirit, experienced by countless numbers of people all through the years since it happened, bears witness that it is true, that it happened as Joseph Smith said it happened, that it was as real as the sunrise over Palmyra, that it is an essential foundation stone, a cornerstone, without which the Church could not be "fitly framed together."

The third cornerstone is the Book of Mormon. I can hold it in my hand. It is real. It has weight and substance that can be physically measured. I can open its pages and read, and it has language both beautiful and uplifting. The ancient record from which it was translated came out of the earth as a voice speaking from the dust. It came as the testimony of generations of men and women who lived upon the earth, who struggled with adversity, who quarreled and fought, who at various times lived the divine law and prospered and at other times forsook God and went down to destruction. It contains what has been described as the fifth Gospel, a moving testament of the new world concerning the visit of the resurrected Redeemer on the soil of the Western Hemisphere.

The evidence for its truth, for its validity in a world that is prone to demand evidence, lies not in archaeology or anthropology, though these may be helpful to some. It lies not in word research or historical analysis, though these may be confirmatory. The evidence for its truth and validity lies within the covers of the book itself. The test of its truth lies in reading it. It is a book of God. Reasonable individuals may sincerely question its origin, but those who read it prayerfully may come to know by a power beyond their natural senses that it is true, that it contains the word of God, that it outlines saving truths of the everlasting gospel, that it came forth by the gift and power of God "to the convincing of the Jew and Gentile that Jesus is the Christ." (Book of Mormon title page.)

The Book of Mormon is here. It must be explained. It can be explained only as the translator himself explained its origin. Hand in hand with the Bible, whose companion volume it is, it stands as another witness to a doubting generation that Jesus is the Christ, the Son of the living God. It is an unassailable cornerstone of our faith.

Cornerstone number four is the restoration to earth of priesthood power and authority. That authority was given to men anciently, the lesser authority to the sons of Aaron to administer in things temporal as well as in some sacred ecclesiastical ordinances. The higher priesthood was given by the Lord himself to his apostles when he declared, "I will give unto thee the keys of the kingdom of heaven: and whatsoever thou shalt bind on earth shall be bound in heaven: and whatsoever thou shalt loose on earth shall be loosed in heaven." (Matthew 16:19.)

In its full restoration, the priesthood involved the coming of the forerunner of Christ, John the Baptist, whose head was taken to satisfy the whims of a wicked woman, and of Peter, James, and John, who faithfully walked with the Master before his death and who proclaimed his resurrection and divinity following his death. It involved Moses, Elias, and Elijah, each bringing priesthood keys to complete the work of restoring all of the acts and ordinances of previous dispensations in this the great, final "dispensation of the fulness of times."

The priesthood is here. It has been conferred upon us. We act in that authority. We speak as sons of God in the name of Jesus Christ and as holders of this divinely given endowment. We know, for we have seen the power of the priesthood. We have seen the sick healed, the lame made to walk, and the coming of light and knowledge and understanding to those who have been in darkness.

Paul wrote concerning the priesthood: "No man taketh this honour unto himself, but he that is called of God, as was

11

Aaron." (Hebrews 5:4.) We have not acquired it through purchase or bargain. The Lord has given it to men who are considered worthy to receive it, regardless of station in life, the color of their skin, or the nation in which they live. It is the power and the authority to govern in the affairs of the kingdom of God. It is given only by ordination by the laying on of hands by those in authority to do so. The qualification for eligibility is obedience to the commandments of God. There is no power on the earth like it. Its authority extends beyond life, through the veil of death, to the eternities ahead. It is everlasting in its consequences.

These great God-given gifts are the unshakable cornerstones that anchor The Church of Jesus Christ of Latter-day Saints, as well as the individual testimonies and convictions of its members: (1) the reality and the divinity of the Lord Jesus Christ as the Son of God; (2) the sublime vision given to the Prophet Joseph Smith of the Father and the Son, ushering in the "dispensation of the fulness of times"; (3) the Book of Mormon as the word of God speaking in declaration of the divinity of the Savior; and (4) the priesthood of God divinely conferred, to be exercised in righteousness for the blessing of our Father's children. Each of these cornerstones is related to the others, each connected by a foundation of apostles and prophets, all tied to the chief cornerstone, Jesus Christ. On this has been established his church, "fitly framed together," for the blessing of all who will partake of its offering. (Ephesians 2:21.)

So undergirded beneath and fitly framed above, the Church stands as the creation of the Almighty. It is a shelter from the storms of life. It is a refuge of peace for those in distress. It is a house of succor for those in need. It is the conservator of eternal truth and the teacher of the divine will. It is the true and living church of the Master.

CHAPTER 3

"GOD HATH NOT GIVEN US THE SPIRIT OF FEAR"

As I have traveled throughout the world, and through the years of my life, I have met many people who have had problems and anxious concerns. In response to these challenges and concerns, I have often recalled some words that were written long ago by the Apostle Paul. At the time he was probably a prisoner in Rome, "ready to be offered," as he said. (2 Timothy 4:6.) He had been a great missionary, unflagging in his testimony, zealous in his desire to bear testimony of the risen Lord. He knew his days were now numbered, and with great feeling he wrote to a junior companion, Timothy, whom he described as "my dearly beloved son": "Wherefore I put thee in remembrance that thou stir up the gift of God, which is in thee. . . . For God hath not given us the spirit of fear; but of power, and of love, and of a sound mind." (2 Timothy 1:6-7.)

Who among us can say that he or she has not felt fear? I know of no one who has been entirely spared. Some, of course, experience fear to a greater degree than do others. Some are able to rise above it quickly, but others are trapped and pulled down by it and even driven to defeat. We suffer from the fear of ridicule, the fear of failure, the fear of loneliness, the fear of ignorance. Some fear the present, some the future. Some carry a burden of sin and would give almost anything to unshackle themselves from that burden, but fear to change their lives. Let us recognize that fear comes not of God, but rather that this gnawing, destructive element comes from the adversary of truth and righteousness. Fear is the antithesis of faith. It is corrosive in its effects, even deadly.

"For God hath not given us the spirit of fear; but of power, and of love, and of a sound mind." These principles are the great antidotes to the fears that rob us of our strength and sometimes knock us down to defeat. They give us power.

What power? The power of the gospel, the power of truth, the power of faith, the power of the priesthood.

Martin Luther was one of the great and courageous forerunners of the Restoration. I love the words of his magnificent hymn:

> *A mighty fortress is our God,*
> *A tower of strength ne'er failing.*
> *A helper mighty is our God,*
> *O'er ills of life prevailing.*
> *He overcometh all.*
> *He saveth from the Fall.*
> *His might and pow'r are great.*
> *He all things did create*
> *And he shall reign forevermore.*
> *—Hymns,* 1985, no. 68

There is a mighty strength that comes of the knowledge that you and I are sons and daughters of God. Within us is something of divinity. Those who have this knowledge and permit it to influence their lives will not stoop to do mean or cheap or tawdry things. Let us encourage the divinity within us to come to the surface. For example, we need not fear ridicule because of our faith. We all occasionally have felt a little of such ridicule. But there is a power within us that can rise above ridicule, that can, in fact, even turn it to good.

I remember hearing an experience of a high school girl who lived far from the headquarters of the Church and who successfully changed the lives of many of her friends. She and her friends, none of whom were members of the Church, talked about having a party. She spoke out affirmatively, saying, "We can have a lot of fun, and we don't need to drink."

The wonderful thing is that her friends respected her. Furthermore, her strength built strength in others who developed the courage to be responsible and decent and moral because of her example. God has given us the power of the gospel to lift us above our fears.

God has given us the power of truth.

President Joseph F. Smith once declared: "We believe in all truth, no matter to what subject it may refer. No sect or religious denomination [or, I may say, no searcher of truth] in the world possesses a single principle of truth that we do not accept or that we will reject. We are willing to receive all truth, from whatever source it may come; for truth will stand, truth will endure." (*Gospel Doctrine* [Salt Lake City: Deseret Book, 1939], p. 1.)

We have nothing to fear when we walk by the light of eternal truth. But we had better be discerning. Sophistry has a way of masking itself as truth. Half truths are used to mislead under the representation that they are whole truths. Innuendo is often used by enemies of this work as representing truth. Theories and hypotheses are often set forth as if they were confirmed truth, when as a matter of fact such procedure may be the very essence of falsehood.

John Jaques, an English convert to the Church, said it beautifully in these words that we now sing:

> *Then say, what is truth?*
> *'Tis the last and the first,*
> *For the limits of time it steps o'er.*
> *Tho the heavens depart and the earth's fountains burst,*
> *Truth, the sum of existence, will weather the worst,*
> *Eternal, unchanged, evermore.*
> — *Hymns,* 1985, no. 272

15

We need not fear as long as we have in our lives the power that comes from living righteously by the truth that is from God our Eternal Father.

Nor need we fear as long as we have *the power of faith*.

The Church has a host of critics and an army of enemies. They mock that which is sacred. They demean and belittle that which has come from God. They pander to the desires of others who evidently enjoy seeing that which is sacred made to look funny. I cannot think of anything less in harmony with the spirit of Christ than this kind of activity.

We are pained by the desecration of that which to us is holy. But we need not fear. This cause is greater than any man. It will outlast all its enemies. We need only go forward, without fear, by the power of faith. Said the Lord in an early season of this work: "Therefore, fear not, little flock; do good; let earth and hell combine against you, for if ye are built upon my rock, they cannot prevail. . . . Look unto me in every thought; doubt not, fear not. Behold the wounds which pierced my side, and also the prints of the nails in my hands and feet; be faithful, keep my commandments, and ye shall inherit the kingdom of heaven." (D&C 6:34, 36-37.)

Paul wrote to the Corinthians: "Watch ye, stand fast in the faith, quit you like men, be strong." (1 Corinthians 16:13.)

God has given us the power of love.

Love of what? Love for the Lord; love for his work, his cause, and his kingdom; love for people; love for one another. I have seen, time and again, how the love of God can bridge the chasm of fear.

Love for the Church can also lift one above doubt. I recall my collegiate experience more than fifty years ago. In many ways that was a dismal period. It was a time of cynicism and much despair. It was the bottom of the Great Depression. The unemployment rate was above 30 percent when I was graduated in 1932. The United States and the entire world were in desperate straits. It was a time of soup lines and suicides.

Young people of college age are inclined to be a little

16

critical and cynical anyway, but that attitude was compounded in the 1930s by the cynicism of the times. It was easy to wonder about many things, to question things in life, in the world, in the Church, in aspects of the gospel. But it was also a season of gladness and a season of love. Behind such thoughts, there was for me an underlying foundation of love that came from great parents and a good family, a wonderful bishop, devoted and faithful teachers, and the scriptures to read and ponder.

Although in our youth we had trouble understanding many things, there was in our hearts something of a love for God and his great work that carried us above any doubts and fears. We loved the Lord and we loved good and honorable friends. From such love we drew great strength.

How great and magnificent is the power of love to overcome fear and doubt, worry and discouragement.

"God hath not given us the spirit of fear; but . . . of a sound mind."

What did Paul mean by the words "a sound mind"? I think he meant the basic logic of the gospel. To me the gospel is not a great mass of theological jargon. It is a simple and beautiful and logical thing, with one quiet truth following another in orderly sequence. I do not fret over the mysteries. I do not worry whether the heavenly gates swing or slide. I am only concerned that they open. I am not worried that the Prophet Joseph Smith gave a number of versions of the first vision any more than I am worried that there are four different writers of the Gospels in the New Testament, each with his own perceptions, each telling the events to meet his own purpose for writing at the time.

I am more concerned with the fact that God has revealed in this dispensation a great and marvelous and beautiful plan that motivates men and women to love their Creator and their Redeemer, to appreciate and serve one another, to walk in faith on the road that leads to immortality and eternal life.

I am grateful for the marvelous declaration that "the glory of God is intelligence, or, in other words, light and truth."

17

(D&C 93:36.) I am grateful for the mandate given us to seek "out of the best books words of wisdom" and to acquire knowledge "by study and also by faith." (D&C 88:118.)

When I was a college student there were many discussions on the question of organic evolution. I took classes in geology and biology and heard the whole story of Darwinism as it was then taught. I wondered about it. I thought much about it. But I did not let it sway me, for I read what the scriptures said about our origins and our relationship to God. Since then I have become acquainted with what to me is a far more important and wonderful kind of evolution. It is the evolution of men and women as the sons and daughters of God, and of our marvelous potential for growth as children of our Creator. For me, this great principle is set forth in the following verses of revelation: "And that which doth not edify is not of God, and is darkness. That which is of God is light; and he that receiveth light, and continueth in God, receiveth more light; and that light groweth brighter and brighter until the perfect day." (D&C 50:23-24.)

I wish we would ponder these words. They are wonderful in their promise concerning the great potential that lies within each of us, born of a promise that has been planted within us as an expression of God's love for his sons and daughters.

What have any of us to fear regarding our challenges and difficulties in life? "Only fear itself," as U. S. President Franklin D. Roosevelt once said in a different context.

Let us refer again to the tremendously important truths taught by Paul: "For God hath not given us the spirit of fear; but of power, and of love, and of a sound mind." Then he gave his great mandate to Timothy: "Be not thou therefore ashamed of the testimony of our Lord." (2 Timothy 1:7-8.)

May this counsel be as a personal charge to each of us. Let us walk with confidence — never with arrogance — and with quiet dignity in our conviction concerning Jesus Christ, our Savior and Redeemer. Let us find strength in the strength that comes from him. Let us find peace in the peace that is of the very essence of his being. Let us be willing to sacrifice in the spirit of him who gave himself a sacrifice for all men. Let us walk in virtue after his mandate, "Be ye clean, that bear the vessels of the Lord." (Isaiah 52:11.) Let us repent of any wrongdoing, in fulfillment of his commandment that we do so, and then let us seek forgiveness under the mercy he has promised. Let us demonstrate our love for him through service to one another.

CHAPTER 4

THE FATHER, THE SON, AND THE HOLY GHOST

The first article of our faith is the pivotal position of our religion. It is significant that in setting forth the primary elements of our doctrine, the Prophet Joseph put this number one:

"We believe in God, the Eternal Father, and in His Son, Jesus Christ, and in the Holy Ghost."

The preeminence given that declaration is in accord with another statement the Prophet made: "It is the first principle of the gospel to know for a certainty the character of God." (*History of the Church* 6:305.)

These tremendously significant and overarching declarations are in harmony with the words of the Lord in his great intercessory prayer: "And this is life eternal, that they might know thee the only true God, and Jesus Christ, whom thou hast sent." (John 17:3.)

I was handed a tract one day. It was written by a critic, an enemy of the Church whose desire is to undermine the faith of the weak and the unknowing. It repeats fallacies that have been parroted for a century and more. It purports to set forth what you and I, as members of The Church of Jesus Christ of Latter-day Saints, believe. Without wishing to argue with any of our friends of other faiths, many of whom I know and for whom I have the highest regard, I take this occasion

to set forth my position on this most important of all theological subjects.

I believe without equivocation or reservation in God, the
Eternal Father. He is my Father, the Father of my spirit, and
the Father of the spirits of all men. He is the great Creator,
the Ruler of the universe. He directed the creation of this earth
on which we live. In his image man was created. He is personal.
He is real. He is individual. He has "a body of flesh and bones
as tangible as man's." (D&C 130:22.) In the account of the
creation of the earth, God said, "Let us make man in our
image, after our likeness." (Genesis 1:26.)

Could any language be more explicit? Does it demean God,
as some would have us believe, that man was created in his
express image? Rather, it should stir within the heart of every
man and woman a greater appreciation for himself or herself
as a son or daughter of God. Paul's words to the Corinthian
Saints are as applicable to us today as they were to those to
whom he wrote. Said he: "Know ye not that ye are the temple
of God, and that the Spirit of God dwelleth in you? If any
man defile the temple of God, him shall God destroy; for the
temple of God is holy, which temple ye are." (1 Corinthians
3:16-17.)

I remember the occasion of more than fifty years ago when,
as a missionary, I was speaking in an open-air meeting in Hyde
Park, London. As I was presenting my message, a heckler
interrupted to say, "Why don't you stay with the doctrine of
the Bible which says in John [4:24] 'God is a Spirit'?"

I opened my Bible to the verse he had quoted and read
to him the entire verse: "God is a Spirit: and they that worship
him must worship him in spirit and in truth." Then I said,
"Of course God is a spirit, and so are you, in the combination
of spirit and body that makes of you a living being, and so
am I."

Each of us is a dual being of spiritual entity and physical
entity. All know of the reality of death when the body dies,
and each of us also knows that the spirit lives on as an indi-

21

vidual entity and that at some time, under the divine plan made possible by the sacrifice of the Son of God, there will be a reunion of spirit and body. Jesus' declaration that God is a spirit no more denies that he has a body than does the statement that I am a spirit while also having a body.

I do not equate my body with God's in its refinement, in its capacity, in its beauty and radiance. His is eternal. Mine is mortal. But that only increases my reverence for him. I worship him "in spirit and in truth." I look to him as my strength. I pray to him for wisdom beyond my own. I seek to love him with all my heart, might, mind, and strength. His wisdom is greater than the wisdom of all men. His power is greater than the power of nature, for he is the Creator Omnipotent. His love is greater than the love of any other, for his love encompasses all of his children, and it is his work and his glory to bring to pass the immortality and eternal life of his sons and daughters of all generations. (See Moses 1:39.) He "so loved the world, that he gave his only begotten Son, that whosoever believeth in him should not perish, but have everlasting life." (John 3:16.)

This is the Almighty of whom I stand in awe and reverence. It is he to whom I look in fear and trembling. It is he whom I worship and unto whom I give honor and praise and glory. He is my Heavenly Father, who has invited me to come unto him in prayer, to speak with him, with the promised assurance that he will hear and respond.

I thank him for the light and knowledge and understanding he has bestowed upon his children. I thank him for his voice, which has spoken eternal truth with power and promise. I thank him for his revelation of himself as set forth in the Old Testament, and for his declaration, as set forth in the New Testament, at the baptism of his Beloved Son in the waters of Jordan when his voice was heard saying: "This is my beloved Son, in whom I am well pleased." (Matthew 3:17.)

I thank him for his similar declaration on the Mount of Transfiguration when he spoke again to Jesus and the apostles, and angels also, when "after six days Jesus taketh Peter, James, and John his brother, and bringeth them up into an high mountain apart, and was transfigured before them: and his face did shine as the sun, and his raiment was white as the light.

"And, behold, there appeared unto them Moses and Elias talking with him.

"Then answered Peter, and said unto Jesus, Lord, it is good for us to be here: if thou wilt, let us make here three tabernacles; one for thee, and one for Moses, and one for Elias.

"While he yet spake, behold, a bright cloud overshadowed them: and behold a voice out of the cloud, which said, This is my beloved Son, in whom I am well pleased; hear ye him." (Matthew 17:1-5.)

I thank him for that voice again heard when the risen Lord was introduced to the people of this hemisphere with the voice of God declaring, "Behold my Beloved Son, in whom I am well pleased, in whom I have glorified my name." (3 Nephi 11:7.)

I stand in awe and reverence and gratitude for his appearance in this dispensation when, as he introduced the risen Lord to one who had sought him in prayer, the Father declared: "This is My Beloved Son. Hear Him!" (Joseph Smith–History 1:17.)

I believe in the Lord Jesus Christ, the Son of the eternal, living God. I believe in him as the Firstborn of the Father and the Only Begotten of the Father in the flesh. I believe in him as an individual, separate and distinct from his Father. I believe in the declaration of John, who opened his gospel with this majestic utterance:

"In the beginning was the Word, and the Word was with God, and the Word was God. The same was in the beginning with God. . . . And the Word was made flesh, and dwelt among us, (and we beheld his glory, the glory as of the only begotten of the Father), full of grace and truth." (John 1:1-2, 14.)

I believe that he was born of Mary of the lineage of David as the promised Messiah, that he was in very deed begotten

23

of the Father, and that in his birth was the fulfillment of the great prophetic declaration of Isaiah: "For unto us a child is born, unto us a son is given: and the government shall be upon his shoulder: and his name shall be called Wonderful, Counsellor, The mighty God, The everlasting Father, The Prince of Peace." (Isaiah 9:6.)

I believe that in his mortal life he was the one perfect man to walk the earth. I believe that in his words are to be found that light and truth which, if observed, would save the world and bring exaltation to mankind. I believe that in his priesthood rests divine authority — the power to bless, the power to heal, the power to govern in the earthly affairs of God, the power to bind in the heavens that which is bound upon the earth.

I believe that through his atoning sacrifice, the offering of his life on Calvary's hill, he expiated the sins of mankind, relieving us from the burden of sin if we will forsake evil and follow him. I believe in the reality and the power of his resurrection. I believe in the grace of God made manifest through Jesus' sacrifice and redemption, and I believe that through his atonement, without any price on our part, each of us is offered the gift of resurrection from the dead. I believe further that through that sacrifice there is extended to every man and woman, every son and daughter of God, the opportunity for eternal life and exaltation in our Father's kingdom, as we hearken to and obey his commandments.

None so great has ever walked the earth. None other has made a comparable sacrifice or granted a comparable blessing. He is the Savior and the Redeemer of the world. I believe in him. I declare his divinity without equivocation or compromise. I love him. I speak his name in reverence and wonder. I worship him as I worship his Father, in spirit and in truth. I thank him and kneel before his wounded feet and hands and side, amazed at the love he offers me.

God be thanked for his Beloved Son who reached out long ago and said to each of us: "Come unto me, all ye that labour and are heavy laden, and I will give you rest. Take my yoke upon you, and learn of me; for I am meek and lowly in heart: and ye shall find rest unto your souls. For my yoke is easy, and my burden is light." (Matthew 11:28-30.)

He lives, the firstfruits of the Resurrection. I know he lives today as really, as certainly, as individually as he lived when, as the risen Lord, he beckoned his discouraged disciples to "come and dine. . . . And [he] taketh bread, and giveth them, and fish likewise." (John 21:12-13.)

The scripture tells of others to whom he showed himself and with whom he spoke as the living, resurrected Son of God.

Likewise in this dispensation he has appeared, and those who saw him declared: "And now, after the many testimonies which have been given of him, this is the testimony, last of all, which we give of him: That he lives! For we saw him, even on the right hand of God; and we heard the voice bearing record that he is the Only Begotten of the Father—that by him, and through him, and of him, the worlds are and were created, and the inhabitants thereof are begotten sons and daughters unto God." (D&C 76:22-24.)

This is the Christ in whom I believe and of whom I testify.

That knowledge comes from the word of scripture, and that testimony comes by the power of the Holy Ghost. It is a gift, sacred and wonderful, borne by revelation from the third member of the Godhead. I believe in the Holy Ghost as a personage of spirit who occupies a place with the Father and the Son, these three constituting the divine Godhead.

The importance of that place is made clear from the words of the Lord who said: "All manner of sin and blasphemy shall be forgiven unto men: but the blasphemy against the Holy Ghost shall not be forgiven unto men. And whosoever speaketh a word against the Son of man, it shall be forgiven him: but whosoever speaketh against the Holy Ghost, it shall not be forgiven him, neither in this world, neither in the world to come." (Matthew 12:31-32.)

That the Holy Ghost was recognized in ancient times as a member of the Godhead is evident from the conversation between Peter and Ananias when the latter held back a part of the price received from the sale of a piece of land. "But Peter said, Ananias, why hath Satan filled thine heart to lie to the Holy Ghost? . . . Thou hast not lied unto men, but unto God." (Acts 5:3-4.)

The Holy Ghost stands as the third member of the Godhead, the Comforter promised by the Savior, who would teach his followers all things and bring all things to their remembrance, whatsoever he had said unto them. (See John 14:26.)

The Holy Ghost is the Testifier of truth, who can teach mankind things they cannot teach one another. In those great and challenging words of Moroni, a knowledge of the truth of the Book of Mormon is promised "by the power of the Holy Ghost." Moroni then declares, "And by the power of the Holy Ghost ye may know the truth of all things." (Moroni 10:4-5.)

I believe that this power, this gift, is available to us today.

I believe in God, the Eternal Father, and in his Son, Jesus Christ, and in the Holy Ghost.

I was baptized in the name of these three. I was married in the name of these three. I have no question concerning their reality and their individuality. That individuality was made apparent when Jesus was baptized by John in Jordan. There in the water stood the Son of God. His Father's voice was heard declaring his divine Sonship, and the Holy Ghost was manifest in the form of a dove. (See Matthew 3:16-17.)

I am aware that Jesus said that they who had seen him had seen the Father. Could not the same be said by many a son who resembles his parent? When Jesus prayed to the Father, certainly he was not praying to himself! They are distinct beings, but they are one in purpose and effort. They are united as one in bringing to pass the grand, divine plan for the salvation and exaltation of the children of God.

In his great, moving prayer in the garden before his betrayal, Christ pleaded with his Father concerning the apostles, whom he loved, saying: "Neither pray I for these alone, but for them also which shall believe on me through their word; that they all may be one; as thou, Father, art in me, and I in thee, that they also may be one in us." (John 17:20-21.) It is that perfect unity between the Father, the Son, and the Holy Ghost that binds these three into the oneness of the divine Godhead.

Miracle of miracles and wonder of wonders, they are interested in us, and we are the substance of their great concern. They are available to each of us. We approach the Father through the Son. He is our intercessor at the throne of God. How marvelous it is that we may so speak to the Father in the name of the Son, and come to know by the power of the Holy Ghost, as a divine gift, of the living reality of these three who constitute the Godhead.

CHAPTER 5

THE HEALING
POWER OF CHRIST

Recently we were in the city of Bacolod on the island of Negros Occidente, in the Republic of the Philippines. There, to my great surprise, I met a man I had not seen in years. The weather was steamy hot, as it always is in Bacolod, the center of the once-thriving Filipino sugar industry, and my friend was in a short-sleeved white shirt with dark trousers, his shoes shined. His beautiful wife was beside him. I said, "What are you doing here?"

He smiled and replied, "We're doing the Lord's work. We're helping the people. We're missionaries."

"Where do you live?"

"In a little house in Ilollo on the island of Panay. We came over on the ferry for the conference."

I thought of when I had last seen them. It was a few years ago. They then lived in a beautiful home in Scarsdale, New York. He was a widely recognized and honored chemist, with a doctorate in chemical engineering. He worked for one of the big multinational companies headquartered in New York. He was credited with putting together the chemical ingredients of a product now sold around the world, the name of which is known to millions of people and the profit from which has run into many millions of dollars for his company. He was well paid and highly respected.

He was also the president of a stake of The Church of Jesus Christ of Latter-day Saints. He had under his direction a corps of church workers who served faithfully in their local wards, many of whom commuted each day to and from New York City, where they held high and responsible positions in some of the great corporations of America. He was their church leader.

Now he was retired. He and his wife had sold their beautiful home, had given their children what furniture they wanted, and had donated the rest to others. They had disposed of their cars and everything except their clothing, their family photographs, and their family history records. They had made themselves available to the Lord and his church to go wherever they might be sent at their own expense.

They were now in the Philippines Bacolod Mission, working among the wonderful, friendly, brown-skinned people of the area. Unemployment is high in this region, and there is much of misery. But wherever this couple go, they touch for good the lives of those among whom they serve. They are there to heal the suffering people, to teach the gospel of Christ, to give encouragement and strength and hope and faith. They are there to heal wounds of misunderstanding and contention. They are there to bless the sick and to help those with diseased bodies and frustrated minds. Their smile is infectious, their laugh a joy to hear. They are living humbly among the poor, down at the level of the people, but standing straight and tall to lift with strong hands.

This former New York executive and his charming companion are in the service of the Savior, giving their full time, their resources, and their love to bless with healing the lives of many who are discouraged and need help. Here is a retired New Yorker, a man of great learning and recognized capacity, living in a home with few conveniences, a simple little place that would fit in the living room of his former house.

He and his wife are there, with others of their kind. They are two of a band of remarkable and dedicated older missionary

29

couples who minister to the wants of people with numerous problems. They receive no financial compensation. They pay their own way. This world's goods mean little to them; they sold all they had when they left to come to the Philippines. They will stay for as long as they are assigned by the Church to do so. Then they want to go on another mission. They are healers among the people, serving in the cause of the Master Healer.

I have since reflected much on the power of Christ to heal and bless. It was he who said, "I am come that they might have life, and that they might have it more abundantly." (John 10:10.) In a world of sickness and sorrow, of tension and jealousy and greed, there must be much of healing if there is to be life abundant.

The prophet Malachi declared, "Unto you that fear my name shall the Sun of righteousness arise with healing in his wings." (Malachi 4:2.)

That prophecy was fulfilled. Jesus came to earth, the Son of God, with power over life and death. He healed the sick, opened the eyes of the blind, and caused the lame to walk and the dead to rise. He was the man of miracles who "went about doing good." (Acts 10:38.)

"So Jesus came again into Cana of Galilee. . . . And there was a certain nobleman, whose son was sick at Capernaum. When he heard that Jesus was come out of Judea into Galilee, he went unto him, and besought him that he would come down, and heal his son: for he was at the point of death. . . .

"Jesus saith unto him, Go thy way; thy son liveth. And the man believed the word that Jesus had spoken unto him, and he went his way. And as he was now going down, his servants met him, and told him, saying, Thy son liveth." (John 4:46-47, 50-51.)

This, the second recorded miracle wrought by the Master, was followed by other miracles of healing. Christ healed by the power of God, which was within him. That power he gave to his chosen disciples, saying, "And I will give unto thee the keys of the kingdom of heaven." (Matthew 16:19.)

That same power has been restored in this generation. It came through the laying on of hands by Peter, James, and John, who received it from the Lord himself. It was bestowed upon Joseph Smith, the prophet of this dispensation. Its presence is among us. Those who are acquainted with the history of the Church are familiar with the account related by Wilford Woodruff concerning the events of July 22, 1839. Nauvoo at that time was an unhealthy and swampy place. There was much sickness. Joseph was among those who were afflicted. But being filled with the Spirit, he rose from his bed and went out among the sick, healing them and raising them. He then crossed the river to the settlement in Montrose, Iowa. I now refer to the account of Elder Woodruff:

"The first house he visited was that occupied by Elder Brigham Young, the president of the quorum of the twelve, who lay sick. Joseph healed him, then he arose and accompanied the Prophet on his visit to others who were in the same condition. They visited Elder W. Woodruff, also Elders Orson Pratt and John Taylor, all of whom were living in Montrose. They also accompanied him. The next place they visited was the home of Elijah Fordham, who was supposed to be about breathing his last. When the company entered the room the Prophet of God walked up to the dying man, and took hold of his right hand and spoke to him; but Brother Fordham was unable to speak, his eyes were set in his head like glass, and he seemed entirely unconscious of all around him. Joseph held his hand and looked into his eyes in silence for a length of time. A change in the countenance of Brother Fordham was soon perceptible to all present. His sight returned, and upon Joseph asking him if he knew him, he, in a low whisper, answered, 'Yes.' Joseph asked him if he had faith to be healed. He answered, 'I fear it is too late; if you had come sooner I think I would have been healed.' The Prophet said, 'Do you believe in Jesus Christ?' He answered in a feeble voice, 'I do.'

31

Joseph then stood erect, still holding his hand in silence several moments; then he spoke in a very loud voice, saying: 'Brother Fordham, I command you in the name of Jesus Christ to arise from this bed and be made whole.' His voice was like the voice of God, and not of man. It seemed as though the house shook to its very foundations. Brother Fordham arose from his bed and was immediately made whole. His feet were bound in poultices, which he kicked off, then putting on his clothes, he ate a bowl of bread and milk, and followed the Prophet into the street." (As quoted in Joseph Fielding Smith, *Essentials in Church History,* rev. ed. [Salt Lake City: Deseret Book, 1979], pp. 223-24.)

Declared James of old: "Is any sick among you? let him call for the elders of the church; and let them pray over him, anointing him with oil in the name of the Lord: and the prayer of faith shall save the sick, and the Lord shall raise him up; and if he have committed sins, they shall be forgiven him." (James 5:14-15.)

That power to heal the sick is still among us. It is the power of the priesthood of God. It is the authority held by the elders of his church.

We welcome and praise and utilize the marvelous procedures of modern medicine, which have done so much to alleviate human suffering and lengthen human life. We are indebted to the dedicated men and women of science and medicine who have conquered so much of disease, who have mitigated pain, who have stayed the hand of death. We cannot say enough of gratitude for them. Yet they are the first to admit the limitations of their knowledge and the imperfection of their skills in dealing with many matters of life and death. The mighty Creator of the heavens and the earth and all that in them are has given to his servants a divine power that sometimes transcends all the powers and knowledge of mankind. I venture to say that there is scarcely a faithful elder of the Church who could not recount instances in which this healing power has been made manifest in behalf of the sick. It is the healing power of Christ.

And there is much of sickness among us other than that of the body. There is the sickness of sin. One of our national magazines carried an extensive review of a sacrilegious film that was shown in theaters across the world. Letters poured in to the editor. The writer of one of these said: "I am a former alcoholic and adulterer set free by the power of the living Jesus Christ." (*Time*, September 5, 1988, p. 7.)

Legion are those who have testified of the healing power of Christ to lift them from the desolation of sin to higher and nobler living.

There is much of another category of sickness among us. I speak of conflicts, quarrels, and arguments, which are a debilitating disease particularly afflicting families. Where there be such problems, I encourage the individuals to invite the healing power of Christ. To those to whom he spoke on the Mount, Jesus said: "Ye have heard that it hath been said, An eye for an eye, and a tooth for a tooth: but I say unto you, That ye resist not evil: but whosoever shall smite thee on thy right cheek, turn to him the other also. . . . And whosoever shall compel thee to go a mile, go with him twain." (Matthew 5:38-41.)

The application of this principle, difficult to live but wondrous in its curative powers, would have miraculous effects on our troubled homes. It is selfishness that is the cause of most of our misery. It is as a cankering disease. The healing power of Christ, found in the doctrine of going the second mile, would do wonders to still argument and accusation, fault-finding and evil speaking.

The same healing spirit would do wonders for the sickness of our society. The Lord has declared that it is our duty, as those blessed with the healing power of the Master, to "succor the weak, lift up the hands which hang down, and strengthen the feeble knees." (D&C 81:5.)

Great is the healing capacity of those who follow the admonition given by James: "Pure religion and undefiled before God and the Father is this, To visit the fatherless and widows in their affliction, and to keep himself unspotted from the world." (James 1:27.)

We live in an environment where there is much of litigation and conflict, of suing and countersuing. Even here, the powers of healing may be invoked. As a young man I worked with Elder Stephen L Richards, then of the Council of the Twelve. When he came into the First Presidency of the Church, he asked me to assist him with a very delicate and sensitive matter. It was fraught with most grave and serious consequences. After listening to him discuss it, I said, "President Richards, you don't want me; you want a lawyer." He said, "I am a lawyer. I don't want to litigate this. I want to compose it."

We directed our efforts to that end, and wonderful results followed. Money was saved, much of it. Embarrassment was avoided. The work was moved forward without fanfare or headlines. Wounds were closed. The healing powers of the Master, the principles of the gospel of Jesus Christ, were invoked in a delicate and difficult situation to compose what otherwise could have become a catastrophe.

It is not always easy to live by these doctrines when our very natures impel us to fight back. For instance, there are those who have made it the mission of their lives to try to destroy the work of God. It has been so from the beginning of the Church, and now, in recent times, we are seeing more of it with evil accusations, falsehoods, and innuendo designed to embarrass the work and its officers. A natural inclination is to fight back, to challenge these falsehoods and bring action against their perpetrators. But when these inclinations make themselves felt, there arise also the words of the Master healer, who said: "Ye have heard that it hath been said, Thou shalt love thy neighbour, and hate thine enemy. But I say unto you, Love your enemies, bless them that curse you, do good to them that hate you, and pray for them which despitefully use you, and persecute you." (Matthew 5:43-44.)

Most of us have not reached that stage of compassion and love and forgiveness. It is not easy. It requires a self-discipline almost greater than we are capable of. But as we try, we come to know that there is a resource of healing, that there is a mighty power of healing in Christ, and that if we are to be his true servants, we must not only exercise that healing power in behalf of others, but, perhaps more important, inwardly.

I would that the healing power of Christ might spread over the earth and be diffused through our society and into our homes, that it might cure men's hearts of the evil and adverse elements of greed and hate and conflict. I believe it could happen. I believe it must happen. If the lamb is to lie down with the lion, then peace must overcome conflict; healing must mend injury.

Jesus of Nazareth healed the sick among whom he moved. His regenerating power is with us today to be invoked through his holy priesthood. His divine teachings, his incomparable example, his matchless life, his all-encompassing sacrifice will bring healing to broken hearts, reconciliation to those who argue and shout, even peace to warring nations if sought with humility and forgiveness and love.

As members of the Church of Jesus Christ, ours is a ministry of healing, with a duty to bind the wounds and ease the pain of those who suffer. Upon a world afflicted with greed and contention, upon families distressed by argument and selfishness, upon individuals burdened with sin and troubles and sorrows, I invoke the healing power of Christ, giving my witness of its efficacy and wonder. I testify of him who is the great source of healing. He is the Son of God, the Redeemer of the world, "The Sun of Righteousness," who came "with healing in his wings."

Chapter 6

"Whosoever Will Save His Life"

One Sunday morning several years ago, I was in the home of a stake president in a small Idaho town. Before morning prayer, the family read together a few verses of scripture. Among these were the words of Jesus as recorded in John 12:24: "Verily, verily, I say unto you, Except a corn of wheat fall into the ground and die, it abideth alone: but if it die, it bringeth forth much fruit."

No doubt the Master was referring to his own forthcoming death, declaring that except he die, his mission in life would be largely in vain. But I see in these words a further meaning. It seems to me that the Lord is saying to each of us that unless we lose ourselves in the service of others, our lives are largely lived to no real purpose, for he went on to say, "He that loveth his life shall lose it; and he that hateth his life in this world shall keep it unto life eternal." (John 12:25.) Or, as recorded in Luke, "Whosoever shall seek to save his life shall lose it; and whosoever shall lose his life shall preserve it." (Luke 17:33.) In other words, he who lives only unto himself withers and dies, while he who forgets himself in the service of others grows and blossoms in this life and in eternity.

That morning in stake conference, the president with whom I had stayed was released after thirteen years of faithful service. There was a great outpouring of love and appreciation, not because of his wealth, not because of his stature in the business community, but because of the great service he had unselfishly given. Without thought of personal interest, he had driven tens of thousands of miles in all kinds of weather. He had spent literally thousands of hours in the interest of others. He had neglected his personal affairs to assist those who needed his help. And in so doing he had come alive and had become great in the eyes of those he had served.

A new president was installed that morning, and there were many who were proud and happy concerning him; but most proud and most happy was a man who sat at the stake clerk's table, a rural mail carrier by profession. Twelve years earlier, it was he who, with quiet, patient labor, had persuaded his totally inactive neighbor to come back into activity. It would have been so much easier to have let that indifferent neighbor go his own way, and it would have been so much easier for the mail carrier to have lived his own quiet life. But he had put aside his personal interests in the interest of another; and that other person became that Sunday the honored and respected leader of a great stake of Zion. As the people sustained their new president, the man at the clerk's table wept tears of gratitude. In living beyond himself, he had brought to Church activity the man sustained that morning as stake president.

Phillips Brooks once made this significant observation: "How carefully most men creep into nameless graves, while now and again one or two forget themselves into immortality."

I remember visiting a friend in southern India. We had first come to know him twelve years previously when we went there in response to his request that someone come to baptize him. Ten years prior to that request he had found a missionary tract of the Church, but how or by whom he did not know. He wrote to the Church offices in Salt Lake City. Other Church literature was sent to him, which he read. We did not baptize him when first we met him; he was not ready. But we arranged for him to be taught the gospel, and he was baptized some months later.

This man worked as an accountant in a cement plant. His salary was meager. His house was small; it would fit into the front room of many homes. But his heart was large and over-flowing. Out of a great love for others that came from his understanding of the gospel of Jesus Christ, he built a school with his own hands on a piece of ground he bought with his savings. It was a simple, rough building; but studying there were some four hundred poor children, each being brought out of the darkness of illiteracy into the light of learning. What this act of love has meant and will mean in their lives is beyond calculation.

Through this one man's efforts, five small branches of the Church were established in the rural villages of southern India. The members constructed three or four little buildings, neat and clean though sparsely furnished, with concrete floors and no benches to sit on. Over the door of each was a sign, in both English and Tamil, that read "The Church of Jesus Christ of Latter-day Saints." There the people met with us, shared our testimonies, and partook of the sacrament of the Lord's Supper.

There are now some thousands of members of the Church among the vast millions of India. That number will continue to grow as the lengthening shadow of that small beginning.

On that same long journey around the earth, we met an-other friend who once was on the faculty of Brigham Young University. His children were then grown, and he and his wife concluded that rather than retire into idleness — as they could well have done, and as millions of others do — they would find some place in the world where they could help some of our Father's children by teaching them the truths that would save them.

They found such a land. They sold their beautiful home; they sold their car; they left friends and relatives for a distant, less comfortable place. But as they cast their bread upon the waters, the Lord opened opportunities for them to teach and lift and help. No one can foretell the consequences of their pioneering.

As I have thought of this man and woman who left the comforts of home and society and friends at an age when most people want to slow down and take it easy, I have thought of the words of the Lord: "And every one that hath forsaken houses, or brethren, or sisters, or father, or mother, or wife, or children, or lands, for my name's sake, shall receive an hundredfold, and shall inherit everlasting life." (Matthew 19:29.) I have thought the same whenever I meet or hear of other elderly brothers and sisters, single or married, who either volunteer or accept calls to serve the Lord in the missions of the Church.

We need them. The Lord needs them. The people of the earth need them. And those wonderful brothers and sisters also need that blessed experience. For, generally speaking, the most miserable people I know are those who are obsessed with themselves; the happiest people I know are those who lose themselves in the service of others.

I recall visiting a college campus where I heard the usual, commonplace complaining of youth: complaints about the pressures of school—as if it were a burden rather than an opportunity to partake of the knowledge of the earth—complaints about housing and about food. I counseled those young people that if the pressures of school were too heavy, if they felt to complain about their housing and their food, then I could suggest a cure for their problems. I suggested that they lay their books aside for a few hours, leave their rooms, and go visit someone who is old and lonely, or someone sick and discouraged. By and large, I have come to see that if we complain about life, it is because we are thinking only of ourselves.

For many years there was a sign on the wall of a shoe repair shop I patronized. It read, "I complained because I had no shoes until I saw a man who had no feet." The most effective medicine for the sickness of self-pity is to lose ourselves in the service of others.

There are some young women, and even some young men, who worry themselves almost sick over the question of whether they will have opportunity for marriage. Of course marriage is desirable; of course it is to be hoped for and worked for and sought after. But worrying about it will never bring it. In fact, it may have the opposite effect, for there is nothing that dulls a personality so much as a negative outlook. Some of our people may not marry in this life, but they should not forget that life can still be as rich and productive and joyful as anything they can possibly imagine. And the key to that joy will be in giving service to others.

I want to commend those of our people who give so willingly of their time in attending to the sacred work within the temples of the Lord. In temple work is found the very essence of selfless service. In my judgment, one of the miracles of our day is the great consecration of time and effort on the part of hundreds of thousands of busy people in behalf of the dead. Those who are engaged in this service know that out of it all comes a sweet and satisfying feeling. This sweet blessing of the Spirit becomes literally a medicine to cure many of the ailments of our lives. From such experiences we come to realize that only when we serve others do we truly serve the Lord.

The Savior has said in our dispensation, "Verily I say, men should be anxiously engaged in a good cause, and do many things of their own free will, and bring to pass much righteousness." And then he added these significant words: "For the power is in them." (D&C 58:27-28.)

The power is in us, in each of us—the power to do significant acts of service on our own initiative if we will become anxiously engaged.

Emerson said that every great institution is but the lengthened shadow of a great person. I have thought of that as I have recalled some of the people who performed great work in areas where I have had responsibility. When I think of the

Church's present status in Korea, I see it as the lengthened shadow of Dr. Kim and two young men who taught him the gospel while he was a student at Cornell University in Ithaca, New York. These young men stirred within their Korean associate an interest in reading the Book of Mormon. Their interest in him and their activities with him were entirely separate from the reasons for their being at Cornell. All three of them were there working toward advanced degrees that could have consumed every minute of their waking time. But they took the time to teach and to learn; and when the Korean Ph.D. returned to his native land, he took with him his love for the Book of Mormon and for the Church whose services he had attended in New York. Latter-day Saint American servicemen involved in the Korean War had also shared the gospel with some of their Korean associates. Thus, the interest of Dr. Kim, this man of learning and responsibility, was the catalyst that led to the establishment of the work in Korea, including the sending of missionaries from Japan. Dr. Kim is deceased, but the work lives on in splendor, touching for eternal good an ever-increasing number of lives in the "Land of the Morning Calm."

In the Philippines today we have a large and faithful membership with multiple stakes and missions. It is one of the more productive proselyting areas in the world. When the history of the work in the Philippines is written, it must include the story of an enthusiastic young woman from Tooele, Utah, who served with the Red Cross in the Pacific campaign of the Second World War. She married an American army officer, and after the war they established their home in Manila. She did much to teach the gospel to others; she pleaded that missionaries be sent. Her husband had legal work done and did many other things to make it possible for the missionaries to come. It would have been much easier for them to have simply gone along their way, making money and enjoying the fruits of it; but she was unceasing in her efforts and in her pleas.

At the time I had responsibility for the work in Asia, and

41

I carried her pleas to the First Presidency, who, in 1961, authorized the extension of formal missionary work to that land. In the spring of 1961 we held a meeting in the Philippines to begin the work. We had no place to meet and received permission from the American Embassy to do so at the American Military Cemetery on the outskirts of Manila. There, where are solemnly remembered the sacrifices of more than 50,000 men who gave their lives in the cause of freedom, we gathered together at 6:30 in the morning. This sister from Utah played a little portable organ she had carried through the campaigns of the war in the Pacific, and we sang the songs of Zion in a strange land. We bore testimony together and invoked the blessings of heaven on what we were to begin there. Present was one native Filipino member of the Church.

That was the beginning of something marvelous, the commencement of a miracle. The rest is history, discouraging at times and glorious at others. I was there for the area conference held several years ago with President Spencer W. Kimball and others. Some 18,000 members of the Church were assembled in the largest indoor meeting place in the Republic.

I wept as I thought of the earlier years, and I remembered with appreciation the woman who largely forgot her own interests as she relentlessly pursued her dream of the day when the Church would be strong in the land in which she then lived, bringing happiness of a kind previously unknown to thousands of wonderful people.

But, you may say, if we were in an exotic place like the Philippines, we would do likewise. I believe that is true. But let me say that every place in the world is exotic, or commonplace, to someone else. In any land, in any city, in any home, in any life, there are opportunities all around to stretch our lives and our interests in behalf of others.

My plea is that if we want joy in our hearts, if we want the Spirit of the Lord in our lives, let us forget ourselves and reach out. Let us put in the background our own personal, selfish interests and reach out in service to others. In so doing, we will find the truth of the Master's great promise of glad tidings:

"Whosoever will save his life, shall lose it; or whosoever will save his life, shall be willing to lay it down for my sake; and if he is not willing to lay it down for my sake, he shall lose it. But whosoever shall be willing to lose his life for my sake, and the gospel, the same shall save it." (JST Mark 8:37-38.)

CHAPTER 7

"AND THE GREATEST OF THESE IS LOVE"

When I was a little boy, we children traded paper hearts at school on Valentine's Day. At night we dropped them at the doors of our friends, stamping on the porch and then running in the dark to hide.

Almost without exception those valentines had printed on them, "I love you." I have since come to know that love is more than a paper heart. Love is the very essence of life. It is the pot of gold at the end of the rainbow. Yet it is more than the end of the rainbow. Love is at the beginning also, and from it springs the beauty that arches across the sky on a stormy day. Love is the security for which children weep, the yearning of youth, the adhesive that binds marriage, and the lubricant that prevents devastating friction in the home; it is the peace of old age, the sunlight of hope shining through death. How rich are those who enjoy it in their associations with family, friends, church, and neighbors.

I am one who believes that love, like faith, is a gift of God. I agree with the expression from author Pearl Buck, "Love cannot be forced, love cannot be coaxed and teased."

In our youth, we sometimes acquire faulty ideas of love, believing that it can be imposed or simply created for convenience. I noted the following in a newspaper column some years ago:

"One of the grand errors we tend to make when we are young is supposing that a person is a bundle of qualities, and we add up the individuals' good and bad qualities, like a bookkeeper working on debits and credits. If the balance is favorable, we may decide to take the jump [into marriage]. . . . The world is full of unhappy men and women who married because . . . it seemed to be a good investment.

"Love, however, is not an investment; it is an adventure. And when marriage turns out to be as dull and comfortable as a sound investment, the disgruntled party soon turns elsewhere. . . . Ignorant people are always saying, 'I wonder what he sees in her,' not realizing that what he sees in her (and what no one else can see) is the secret essence of love." (Sydney J. Harris, *Deseret News*.)

I think of two friends from my high school and university years. He was a boy from a country town, plain in appearance, without money or apparent promise. He had grown up on a farm, and if he had any quality that was attractive, it was the capacity to work. He carried bologna sandwiches in a brown paper bag for his lunch and swept the school floors to pay his tuition. But with all of his rustic appearance, he had a smile and a personality that seemed to sing of goodness. She was a city girl who had come out of a comfortable home. She would not have won a beauty contest, but she was wholesome in her decency and integrity and attractive in her decorum and dress.

Something wonderful took place between them. They fell in love. Some whispered that there were far more promising boys for her, and a gossip or two noted that perhaps other girls might have interested him. But these two laughed and danced and studied together through their school years. They married when people wondered how they could ever earn enough to stay alive. He struggled through his professional school and came out well in his class. She scrimped and saved and worked and prayed. She encouraged and sustained, and when things were really tough, she said quietly, "Somehow we can make it." Buoyed by her faith in him, he kept going

45

through these difficult years. Children came, and together they loved them and nourished them and gave them the security that came of their own love for and loyalty to each other. Now many years have passed. Their children are grown, a lasting credit to them, to the Church, and to the communities in which they live.

I remember seeing this couple on a plane as I returned from an assignment. I walked down the aisle in the semidarkness of the cabin and saw a woman, white-haired, her head on her husband's shoulder as she dozed. His hand was clasped warmly about hers. He was awake and recognized me. She awakened, and we talked. They were returning from a convention where he had delivered a paper before a learned society. He said little about it, but she proudly spoke of the honors accorded him.

I wish that I might have caught with a camera the look on her face as she talked of him. Forty-five years earlier people without understanding had asked what they saw in each other. I thought of that as I returned to my seat on the plane. Their friends of those days saw only a farm boy from the country and a smiling girl with freckles on her nose. But these two found in each other love and loyalty, peace and faith in the future. There was a flowering in them of something divine, planted there by that Father who is our God. In their school days they had lived worthy of that flowering of love. They had lived with virtue and faith, with appreciation and respect for self and one another. In the years of their difficult professional and economic struggles, they had found their greatest earthly strength in their companionship. Now in mature age, they were finding peace and quiet satisfaction together. Beyond all this, they were assured of an eternity of joyful association through priesthood covenants long since made and promises long since given in the House of the Lord.

There are other great and necessary expressions of the gift of love.

"Then one of them, which was a lawyer, asked [Jesus] a

question, tempting him, and saying, Master, which is the great commandment in the law? Jesus said unto him, Thou shalt love the Lord thy God with all thy heart, and with all thy soul, and with all thy mind. This is the first and great commandment. And the second is like unto it, Thou shalt love thy neighbour as thyself. On these two commandments hang all the law and the prophets." (Matthew 22:35-40.)

Who is my neighbor? To answer this, we need only read the moving parable of the Good Samaritan, or the word of the Lord concerning the day of judgment when "the King [shall] say unto them on his right hand, Come ye blessed of my Father, inherit the kingdom prepared for you from the foundation of the world: For I was an hungred, and ye gave me meat: I was thirsty, and ye gave me drink: I was a stranger, and ye took me in: naked, and ye clothed me: I was sick, and ye visited me: I was in prison, and ye came unto me.

"Then shall the righteous answer him, saying, Lord, when saw we thee an hungred, and fed thee? or thirsty, and gave thee drink? When saw we thee a stranger, and took thee in? or naked, and clothed thee? Or when saw we thee sick, or in prison, and came unto thee?

"And the King shall answer and say unto them, Verily I say unto you, Inasmuch as ye have done it unto one of the least of these my brethren, ye have done it unto me." (Matthew 25:34-40.)

The greatest challenge we face in our hurried, self-centered lives is to follow this counsel of the Master.

Years ago I read the story of a young woman who went into a rural area as a schoolteacher. Among those in her class was a girl who had failed before and who was failing again. The student could not read. She came from a family without means to take her to a larger city for examination to determine whether she had a problem that could be remedied. Sensing that the difficulty might lie with the girl's eyes, the young teacher, at her own expense, arranged to take the student to have her eyes tested. A deficiency was discovered that could be

47

corrected with glasses. Soon an entire new world opened to the student. For the first time in her life, she saw clearly the words before her. The salary of that country schoolteacher was meager, but out of the little she had, she made an investment that completely changed the life of a failing student, and in doing so she found a new dimension in her own life.

Every returned missionary can recount experiences of losing oneself in the service of others and finding that to be the most rewarding experience of his or her life. Every member of the Church actively involved in service to God and others can recount similar stories, as can devoted parents and marriage partners who have given of their time and means, and have loved and sacrificed so greatly that their concern for each other and their children has known almost no bounds.

Love is the only force that can erase the differences between people, that can bridge chasms of bitterness. I recall these lines by Edwin Markham:

> *Hate drew a circle that shut me out—*
> *Heretic, rebel, a thing to flout.*
> *But Love and I had the wit to win:*
> *We drew a circle that took him in.*

He who most beautifully taught this everlasting truth was the Son of God, the one perfect exemplar and teacher of love. His coming to earth was an expression of his Father's love. "For God so loved the world, that he gave his only begotten Son, that whosoever believeth in him should not perish, but have everlasting life. For God sent not his Son into the world to condemn the world; but that the world through him might be saved." (John 3:16-17.)

The Savior spoke prophetically of that sacrifice and of the love that culminated in his redemptive sacrifice when he declared, "Greater love hath no man than this, that a man lay down his life for his friends." (John 15:13.)

To all of us who would be his disciples, he has given the great commandment, "A new commandment I give unto you,

48

That ye love one another; as I have loved you, that ye also love one another." (John 13:34.)

If the world is to be improved, the process of love must make a change in the hearts of mankind. It can do so when we look beyond self to give our love to God and others, and do so with all our heart, with all our soul, and with all our mind.

The Lord has declared in modern revelation, "If your eye be single to my glory, your whole bodies shall be filled with light, and there shall be no darkness in you." (D&C 88:67.)

As we look with love and gratitude to God, as we serve him with an eye single to his glory, there goes from us the darkness of sin, the darkness of selfishness, the darkness of pride. There will come an increased love for our Eternal Father and for his Beloved Son, our Savior and our Redeemer. There will come a greater sense of service toward our fellowmen, less of thinking of self and more of reaching out to others. This principle of love is the basic essence of the gospel of Jesus Christ. Without love of God and love of neighbor there is little else to commend the gospel to us as a way of life.

Paul the Apostle spoke well these words: "Though I speak with the tongues of men and of angels, and have not [love], I am become as sounding brass, or a tinkling cymbal. And though I have the gift of prophecy, and understand all mysteries, and all knowledge; and though I have all faith, so that I could remove mountains, and have not [love], I am nothing. . . .[Love] never faileth: but whether there be prophecies, they shall fail; whether there be tongues, they shall cease; whether there be knowledge, it shall vanish away." (1 Corinthians 13:1-2, 8.)

The Master taught: "For whosoever will save his life shall lose it: but whosoever will lose his life for my sake, the same shall save it." (Luke 9:24.)

This remarkable and miraculous process occurs in our own lives as we reach out with love to serve others. Each of us can, with effort, successfully root the principle of love deep in our being so that we may be nourished by its great power all of our lives. For as we tap into the power of love, we will come to understand the great truth written by John: "God is love; and he that dwelleth in love dwelleth in God." (1 John 4:16.)

CHAPTER 8

WE HAVE
A WORK TO DO

I invite members of the Church to consider anew the great mandate given by the Lord to all who desire to be known as his disciples. It is a mandate we cannot dodge, and one from which we cannot shrink. That mandate is to teach the gospel to the nations and peoples of the earth.

This was the final charge given by the Lord following his resurrection and before his ascension. It was repeated at the opening of this dispensation. Following the organization of the first Quorum of the Twelve in 1835, Oliver Cowdery, counselor in the First Presidency, delivered a charge to these men. That statement has become something of a charter for all members of the Twelve who have succeeded that first group. In that charge is the following counsel: "Be zealous to save souls. The soul of one man is as precious as the soul of another. . . . The Gospel must roll forth, and it will until it fills the whole earth. . . . You have a work to do that no other men can do; you must proclaim the Gospel in its simplicity and purity; and we commend you to God and the word of His grace." (*History of the Church* 2:196-98.)

Subsequent to that counsel, the Lord gave the revelation known as section 112 of the Doctrine and Covenants, which was directed to the Twelve. In it are these words: "Contend thou, therefore, morning by morning; and day after day let thy warning voice go forth; and when the night cometh let not the inhabitants of the earth slumber, because of thy speech. . . . And I will be with you; and in whatsoever place ye shall proclaim my name an effectual door shall be opened unto you, that they may receive my word." (D&C 112:5, 19.)

At the outset, missionaries were sent into the surrounding areas, into Canada, and in 1837 across the sea to England. It was in the Kirtland Temple that the Prophet Joseph Smith spoke to Elder Heber C. Kimball: "Brother Heber, the spirit of the Lord has whispered to me: 'Let my servant Heber go to England and proclaim my gospel and open the door of salvation to that nation.'"

Then came Elder Kimball's acknowledgment of his fear. Exclaiming in self-humiliation, he said: "O, Lord, I am a man of stammering tongue, and altogether unfit for such a work; how can I go to preach in that land, which is so famed throughout Christendom for learning, knowledge and piety; the nursery of religion; and to a people whose intelligence is proverbial!" (Orson F. Whitney, *Life of Heber C. Kimball* [Salt Lake City: Bookcraft, 1945], p. 104.)

But Elder Kimball and his associates went to England. While the language they found was essentially the same as their own, many of the customs they met were different. However, they paid little attention to these. Their message was the gospel of salvation. They spoke of little else. And history bears remarkable testimony to the success of their labors. In the years that immediately followed, the message of the restored gospel was taken to the isles of the sea, where entirely new and unique cultures were encountered. It was so in the lands of Europe, with new languages to be learned and new customs to be confronted.

After the Saints went west, even though they were faced with the tremendous tasks of subduing the wilderness and building a commonwealth, they did not slacken their efforts to carry the gospel to the nations of the earth. In the conference held in 1852, men were called from the congregation to go not only to the lands of Europe, but to China and Siam (now Thailand). It is stirring to note that in those pioneering days, missionaries were sent to India, where today, after a long lapse, we are again planting gospel seeds.

I marvel at the boldness — rather, I prefer to characterize it as the *faith* — of the leaders and members of the Church in that pioneering era to stretch their relatively small membership and their thin resources so far in carrying the gospel to distant lands. One cannot read Elder Parley P. Pratt's account of his travels to Chile without recognizing with gratitude the courage and the faith of those early missionaries, who took with such seriousness the Lord's charge to carry the gospel to the nations of the earth. Their long journeys across the seas were made under extremely adverse circumstances. When they stepped ashore, there was neither friend nor companion to meet them. They had no briefing concerning the conditions they were to meet, no knowledge of the languages of the people among whom they were to labor. Many of them became sick as their bodies struggled to adapt to the food and other circumstances of living. But they were filled with a sense of mission, commanded by a charge to take the gospel of salvation to the peoples of the earth. The cultures they encountered created challenges for them, but these were only incidental to their larger responsibility.

Think of how conditions have changed from the mid-nineteenth century to those of today, making easier the flow of the gospel throughout the world. First, it is apparent to all that we live in a rapidly shrinking world. Weeks, even months, were once required to travel across the Pacific. Today we can board a luxurious giant aircraft in San Francisco in the evening, and ten hours later pass through immigration and customs formalities in Tokyo, having enjoyed a good meal en route. We cannot dismiss lightly the importance of the vast traffic of airliners crossing the trade routes of the world and the effects of such interaction among nations insofar as cultural differences are concerned.

Second, as the educational level rises throughout the world, there is a greater understanding and appreciation of other peoples worldwide. There is so much information now available to all who want to visit another land that they need not go in ignorance of what they will find there. Furthermore, they will discover among the peoples they visit a rather extensive knowledge of the culture from which they have come. International broadcasting and the great news services in the world have brought Paris and Pretoria into our living rooms. We are made almost instantly aware of significant happenings in New Delhi, Buenos Aires, and other areas worldwide.

Third, there is an increasing knowledge of languages among the people of the earth. Not only is English spoken almost everywhere in major cities — perhaps not spoken well, yet it is understandable — but our missionaries also go out with considerable ability to communicate in the tongue in which they will announce the gospel message to those they meet. We have taken giant steps forward in facilitating the teaching of the gospel in other lands through the establishment of Church language training centers. These facilities are unsurpassed anywhere in the world.

Another factor that substantially blesses missionaries so that they may be productive in their sacred service is the caliber of the men who are presiding over the missions. Those who serve in these capacities are not novices; they and their wives are mature brothers and sisters of broad experience. They stand as leaders and advisers, teaching younger missionaries and counseling older couples who come to them, protecting them from pitfalls into which they might stumble.

Finally, I note the tremendous growth of understanding that exists in many parts of the earth concerning that which unites us all as children of our Father in heaven. To me, the people in Asia look much the same and act in similar ways as people at home. That is, people are essentially the same in our own cultures as they are outside our cultures. For instance, I think of such common denominators, found among all people, as love of husband and wife, love between parents and children, appreciation for beauty in whatever form it is found, concern about suffering, recognition of leadership, acknowledgment of a higher power to whom we may appeal for help and who sits in judgment upon us all, an ever-present conscience, and a sense of right and wrong.

Years ago I was asked whether the missionary lessons we use in the Orient are substantially different from those we use in countries where the people are primarily Christians. I responded that we use essentially the same lessons because we teach the same kind of people whose hearts are touched by the same eternal truths. I stated further that the people of Asia are children of God, just as are the people of the United States, and because we have all come of the same parentage, we respond to the same truth. The fact that one's skin may be of a slightly different color, that one's eyes may have a slightly different set, that one may wear a different type of clothing does not in any sense make of him or her a different kind of individual. People the world over respond to the same stimuli in essentially the same way. They seek warmth when they are cold; they know the same kinds of pain; they experience sadness; and they know joy. And everywhere, people look to a superior power. They may call him by various names, and they may describe him in various ways, but they are aware of his being and look to him for strength beyond their own.

When differences — either with our neighbors or in other cultures — seem to stand as hurdles as we seek to share the gospel, quiet courtesy usually removes these hurdles. As we keep the Lord's commandment to introduce the gospel to others, I testify that the Spirit of the Lord helps overcome the differences between those who teach and those who are taught. The Lord made the process clear when he said, "Wherefore, he that preacheth [by the Spirit] and he that receiveth [by the Spirit], understand one another, and both are edified and rejoice together." (D&C 50:22.)

I am satisifed that the most effective means each of us has

in our calling to share the gospel is the Spirit of the Lord. We have all seen it in others. As we do the Lord's work, we have also sensed it in ourselves. On such occasions, superficial differences between us and those we teach seem to fall like scales from our eyes. (See 2 Nephi 30:6.) A warmth of kinship and understanding emerges that is marvelous to behold. We literally understand one another, and we literally are edified and rejoice together.

Truly we are engaged in a marvelous work and a wonder. We now have missions and missionaries in the lands of North, Central, and South America, most of the countries in Europe, in many nations of Asia, and in the islands of the Pacific, and the restored gospel is being carried into yet other lands. The results are marvelous to behold. Regardless of the nation in which they are found, Latter-day Saints speak with the same voice and bear testimony of the same eternal truths and with the same fervency of spirit. The cost has been and is great in terms of sacrifice, devotion, and labor, but the results are a miracle to witness.

Now even greater challenges lie ahead for the future. One cannot think of the hundreds of millions who have never heard of this work without wondering how our charge to teach all mankind can ever be accomplished. There are nations where we presently cannot legally go. We honor and obey the laws of these nations. But if we will be both alert and patient, the Lord will open the way in the appropriate season. His is the timetable. Meanwhile, there is much to be done with those immediately around us. As we put forth our effort and pray humbly for inspiration, we will be blessed in our desires to share the gospel with our families, friends, neighbors, and acquaintances.

The progress of the Church in our day is truly astounding. The God of heaven has brought to pass this latter-day miracle, and what we have seen is but a foretaste of greater things yet to come. The work will be accomplished by humble men and women, young and old, who will do it because they believe in the word of the Lord when he said: "And any that shall go and preach this gospel of the kingdom, and fail not to continue faithful in all things, shall not be weary in mind, neither darkened, neither in body, limb, nor joint; and a hair of [their] head shall not fall to the ground unnoticed. And they shall not go hungry, neither athirst." (D&C 84:80.)

The word will succeed because it is the Lord who has promised: "And whoso receiveth you, there I will be also, for I will go before your face. I will be on your right hand and on your left, and my Spirit shall be in your hearts, and mine angels round about you, to bear you up." (D&C 84:88.)

With our charge divinely given, with blessings divinely promised, let us go forward in faith. As we do so, the Lord will bless our efforts. Let us do our part in sharing the gospel with those around us, by example first and then by inspired precept.

The stone cut out of the mountain without hands will continue to roll forth until it has filled the whole earth. (See Daniel 2.) I give you my witness of this truth and of the truth that each of us can help in ways that are appropriate to our circumstances if we will seek the guidance and inspiration of our Father in heaven. This is God's work that we do, and with his blessing we shall not fail.

CHAPTER 9

BUILDING FAITH
THROUGH THE
BOOK OF MORMON

We often sing a favorite hymn, the words written well over a century ago by Parley P. Pratt:

> *An angel from on high*
> *The long, long silence broke;*
> *Descending from the sky,*
> *These gracious words he spoke:*
> *Lo! in Cumorah's lonely hill*
> *A sacred record lies concealed.*
> *Lo! in Cumorah's lonely hill*
> *A sacred record lies concealed.*
> — *Hymns,* 1985, no. 13

These words represent Elder Pratt's declaration of the miraculous coming forth of a most remarkable book. Permit me to tell you how he came to know of the book about which he wrote.

In August 1830, as a lay preacher, Parley Parker Pratt was traveling from Ohio to eastern New York. At Newark, along the Erie Canal, he left the boat and walked ten miles into the country. There he met a Baptist deacon by the name of Hamlin, who told him "of a *book,* a STRANGE BOOK, a VERY STRANGE BOOK!" Elder Pratt continued: "This book,

[Hamlin] said, purported to have been originally written on plates either of gold or brass, by a branch of the tribes of Israel; and to have been discovered and translated by a young man near Palmyra, in the State of New York, by the aid of visions, or the ministry of angels. I inquired of him how or where the book was to be obtained. He promised me the perusal of it, at his house the next day. . . . Next morning I called at his house, where, for the first time, my eyes beheld the 'BOOK OF MORMON' — that book of books . . . which was the principal means, in the hands of God, of directing the entire course of my future life.

"I opened it with eagerness, and read its title page. I then read the testimony of several witnesses in relation to the manner of its being found and translated. After this I commenced its contents by course. I read all day; eating was a burden, I had no desire for food; sleep was a burden when the night came, for I preferred reading to sleep.

"As I read, the spirit of the Lord was upon me, and I knew and comprehended that the book was true, as plainly and manifestly as a man comprehends and knows that he exists." (*Autobiography of Parley P. Pratt* [Salt Lake City: Deseret Book, 1938], pp. 36-37.)

Parley Pratt was then twenty-three years of age. Reading the Book of Mormon affected him so profoundly that he was soon baptized into the Church and became one of its most effective and powerful advocates. In the course of his ministry he traveled from coast to coast across what is now the United States, into Canada, and to England; he also directed the opening of the work in the isles of the Pacific and was the first Mormon elder to set foot on the soil of South America. In 1857, while serving a mission in Arkansas, he was killed by an assailant. He was buried in a rural area near the community of Alma, and today in that quiet place a large block of polished granite marks the site of his grave. Incised in its surface are the words of another of his great and prophetic hymns, setting forth his vision of the work in which he was engaged:

The morning breaks, the shadows flee;
Lo, Zion's standard is unfurled! . . .
The dawning of a brighter day
Majestic rises on the world.

The clouds of error disappear
Before the rays of truth divine; . . .
The glory bursting from afar
Wide o'er the nations soon will shine.
—Hymns, 1985, no. 1

Parley Pratt's experience with the Book of Mormon was not unique. As the volumes of the first edition were circulated and read, strong men and women by the hundreds were so deeply touched that they gave up everything they owned, and in the years that followed, not a few gave their lives for the witness they carried in their hearts of the truth of this remarkable volume.

Today it is more widely read than at any time in its history. Whereas there were five thousand copies in that first edition, today's editions are ordered in lots of as many as a million, and the book currently is printed in more than eighty languages. Its appeal is as timeless as truth, as universal as mankind. It is the only book that contains within its covers a promise that by divine power the reader may know with certainty of its truth. Its origin is miraculous; when the story of that origin is first told to one unfamiliar with it, it is almost unbelievable. But the book is here to be felt and handled and read. No one can dispute its presence.

All efforts to account for its origin, other than the account given by Joseph Smith, have been shown to lack substance. It is a record of ancient America. It is the scripture of the New World, as certainly as the Bible is the scripture of the Old. Each speaks of the other. Each carries with it the spirit of inspiration, the power to convince and to convert. Together they become two witnesses, hand in hand, that Jesus is the Christ, the resurrected and living Son of the living God.

Its narrative is a chronicle of nations long since gone. But in its descriptions of the problems of today's society, it is as current as the morning newspaper and much more definitive, inspired, and inspiring concerning the solutions to those problems.

I know of no other writing that sets forth with such clarity the tragic consequences to societies that follow courses contrary to the commandments of God. Its pages trace the stories of two distinct civilizations that flourished on the Western Hemisphere. Each began as a small nation, its people walking in the fear of the Lord. Each prospered, but with prosperity came growing evils. The people succumbed to the wiles of ambitious and scheming leaders who oppressed them with burdensome taxes, who lulled them with hollow promises, who countenanced and even encouraged loose and lascivious living, who led them into terrible wars that resulted in the death of millions and the final extinction of two great civilizations in two different eras.

No other written testament so clearly illustrates the fact that when men and nations walk in the fear of God and in obedience to his commandments, they prosper and grow; but when they disregard him and his word, there comes a decay which, unless arrested by righteousness, leads to impotence and death. The Book of Mormon is an affirmation of the Old Testament proverb, "Righteousness exalteth a nation: but sin is a reproach to any people." (Proverbs 14:34.)

While the Book of Mormon speaks with power about the issues that affect our modern society, the great and stirring burden of its message is a testimony, vibrant and true, that Jesus is the Christ, the promised Messiah. The book bears witness of him who walked the dusty roads of Palestine healing the sick and teaching the doctrines of salvation; who died upon the cross of Calvary; who on the third day came forth from the tomb, appearing to many; and who, as a resurrected being, visited the people of the Western Hemisphere, concerning whom he earlier had said: "Other sheep I have, which are not of this fold: them also I must bring, and they shall hear my voice; and there shall be one fold, and one shepherd." (John 10:16.)

For centuries the Bible stood alone as a written testimony of the divinity of Jesus of Nazareth. Now, at its side, stands a second and powerful witness to lead mankind to the Lord.

I recall hearing an officer of the United States Air Force stand before a group and tell of the circumstances surrounding his coming into the Church. He said: "I had a date with a lovely young woman. When I called on her, I noticed on the table a copy of the Book of Mormon. I had never heard of it before. I began to read. I became interested. I secured a copy of the book and read it through. I had only the traditional idea of God and Jesus Christ. I had never given serious thought to the matter. But as I read this book there came into my mind light and understanding of eternal truths, and into my heart a testimony that God is our Eternal Father, and that Jesus is our Savior."

This man's experience with the Book of Mormon is similar to that of millions of others who have been influenced by it. The same book that converted Brigham Young, Willard Richards, Orson and Parley Pratt, and many other leaders of the Church in its early years is converting people today in Argentina, in Finland, in Spain, in Taiwan, in Tonga, and wherever else individuals are reading it prayerfully and with real intent. The promise of Moroni, written in his loneliness following the destruction of his people, is being fulfilled every day. (See Moroni 10:4-5.)

Each time we encourage others to read the Book of Mormon, we do them a favor. If they will read it prayerfully and with a sincere desire to know the truth, they will know by the power of the Holy Ghost that the book is true. From that knowledge will flow a conviction of the truth of many other things. For if the Book of Mormon is true, then God lives. Testimony upon testimony runs through its pages of the solemn fact that our Father is real, that he is personal, and that he loves his children and seeks their happiness.

If the Book of Mormon is true, then Jesus is the Son of God, the Only Begotten of the Father in the flesh, born of Mary, "a virgin, most beautiful . . . above all other virgins" (see 1 Nephi 11:13-21), for the book so testifies in a description unexcelled in all literature.

If the Book of Mormon is true, then Jesus is verily our Redeemer, the Savior of the world. The great purpose of its preservation and coming forth, according to its own statement, is "to the convincing of the Jew and Gentile that Jesus is the Christ, the Eternal God, manifesting himself unto all nations." (Title Page.)

If the Book of Mormon is true, then America is a choice land, but if it is to remain such, the inhabitants of the land must worship the God of the land, the Lord Jesus Christ. The histories of two great nations, told with warning in this sacred volume, indicate that while we must have science, while we must have education, while we must have arms, we also must have righteousness if we are to merit the protection of God.

If the Book of Mormon is true, Joseph Smith was a prophet of God, for he was the instrument in the hands of God in bringing to light this testimony of the divinity of our Lord.

If this book is true, the President of the Church is a prophet of God, for he holds all of the keys, gifts, powers, and authority held by the Prophet Joseph, who brought forth this latter-day work.

If the Book of Mormon is true, the Church is true, for the same authority under which this sacred record came to light is present and manifest among us today. It is a restoration of the church set up by the Savior in Palestine. It is a restoration of the church set up by the Savior when he visited the Western Hemisphere as set forth in this sacred record.

If the Book of Mormon is true, the Bible is true. The Bible is the Testament of the Old World; the Book of Mormon is the Testament of the New. One is the record of Judah; the other is the record of Joseph, and they have come together in the hand of the Lord in fulfillment of the prophecy of Ezekiel. (Ezekiel 37:19.) Together they declare the Kingship of the Redeemer of the world and the reality of his kingdom.

Here is a voice that has touched the hearts of people in many lands. Those who have read it prayerfully, be they rich or poor, learned or unlearned, have grown under its power.

Let me tell you of a letter we received some years ago. A man wrote, saying, "I am in a federal prison. I recently came across a copy of the Book of Mormon in the prison library. I read it, and when I read Mormon's lamentation over his fallen people — 'O ye fair ones, how could ye have departed from the ways of the Lord! O ye fair ones, how could ye have rejected that Jesus, who stood with open arms to receive you! Behold, if ye had not done this, ye would not have fallen' (Mormon 6:17-18) — I felt that Mormon was talking to me. Can I get a copy of that book?"

We sent him a copy. Some time later, he walked into my office a changed man. He was touched by the spirit of the Book of Mormon and today is a successful man, rehabilitated, earning a living honestly for himself and his family.

Such is the power of this great book in the lives of those who read it prayerfully. Without reservation I promise you that if you will prayerfully read the Book of Mormon, regardless of how many times you have previously read it, there will come into your heart an added measure of the Spirit of the Lord. There will come a strengthened resolution to walk in obedience to his commandments, and there will come a stronger testimony of the living reality of the Son of God.

CHAPTER 10

THE ENVIRONMENT OF OUR HOMES

What a difficult, at times discouraging, but nevertheless wonderful and challenging thing it is to be a parent—a mother, a father of children born and growing in this complex age. We all make mistakes; most of us make many of them. We all experience heartache, and most of us have felt much of that. But we have also felt pride and gladness as we have witnessed our children grow from infancy to maturity.

It is not an easy thing to be a parent. There is so much of frustration, so much of worry, so much of blighted dreams and broken hopes for so very many. I recognize, of course, that there are many homes where this is not the case, where things go smoothly and well, where angry voices are never raised, where there are parents who are happy and calm, and children who are faithful and grow up without serious problems. If such be your home, be grateful. Thank the Lord for the marvelous blessing that has come to you.

But I assure you that there are many of the other kind, for I have received letters concerning them—letters from parents and letters from sons and daughters. It is very easy to say that if we will do this or that, all will go well. But I have seen conscientious men and women, people who are faithful and true, people who try to observe the teachings of the Church, who still experience broken hearts over the conduct of their children.

I know some of the answers to these problems, but I confess that I do not know all of them. Many of the problems are of our own making. In other cases, they seem to happen notwithstanding all that we do to guard against them. I think of some wonderful people I know. Their older children grew up and were married and went forward with their lives in a way that made the hearts of their parents glad. And then there was a younger son, a bright and able boy. But the associations he had in high school moved him in another direction. His hair grew long and his dress unkempt. He did other things that brought great distress to his father and mother. His father was distraught. He scolded and threatened; he wept and prayed and rebuked his son. But there was no response. The boy went his wayward course. His mother also wept and prayed. But she controlled her feelings and kept her voice low. She repeatedly expressed to her son her love for him. He left home. She kept his room tidy, his bed made, and food for him in the refrigerator, and she told him that whenever he felt like coming home he would be made welcome.

Months passed while hearts ached. Then the love of his mother finally began to touch his heart. He came back occasionally to sleep. Without ever scolding, she smiled, joked with him, placed delicious food before him, put her arms around him, and expressed her love. Eventually he began to show increasing neatness in his person. He stayed home more. He came to realize that there was no other place as comfortable, no place as secure, no place as happy as that home he had left earlier. He finally got his life under control. He went on a mission, at an age older than most young men do. He proved to be a successful missionary. He returned home, entered college, and began to apply himself. The last time I saw him, he and his mother, each blessed with a good voice, sang a duet while some who knew the history of that family shed tears.

To any who may have such sons or daughters, may I suggest that you never quit trying. They are never lost until you have given up. Remember that it is love, more than any

66

other thing, that will bring them back. Punishment is not likely to do it. Reprimands without love will not accomplish it. Patience, expressions of appreciation, and that strange and remarkable power which comes with prayer will eventually win through.

In the spirit of trying to be helpful, I should like to suggest four elements in building the environment of our homes. I suggest that parents let their children grow in a home where there is (1) a spirit of service, (2) an atmosphere of growth, (3) the discipline of love, and (4) the practice of prayer.

A SPIRIT OF SERVICE

Selfishness is a destructive, gnawing, corrosive element in the lives of most of us. It lies at the root of much of the tension between parents and children, and it leads to strain in well-meaning parents who sometimes nurture harmful selfishness in children by indulging with extravagance their wishes for costly and unneeded things.

The antidote for selfishness is service, a reaching out to those about us — those in the home and those beyond the walls of the home. Children who grow up in homes where parents are selfish and grasping are likely to develop those tendencies in their own lives. On the other hand, children who see their parents forgo comforts for themselves as they reach out to those in distress will likely follow the same pattern when they grow to maturity.

Children who see their parents active in the Church, serving God through service to their fellowman, will likely act in the same spirit when they grow up. Children who see their parents assisting those in distress, succoring the poor, and going to the rescue of those in trouble will likely exemplify that same spirit as they grow in years.

Would you have your children grow in a spirit of unselfishness? Indulgence of selfish desires will not do it. Rather, let them come to see in their own homes, and in their most intimate family associations, the truth of the great principle set forth by the Lord: "Whosoever will save his life shall lose it; but whosoever shall lose his life for my sake and the gospel's, the same shall save it." (Mark 8:35.)

AN ATMOSPHERE OF GROWTH

What a marvelously interesting thing it is to watch young minds stretch and strengthen. I am one who greatly appreciates the vast potential of television for good. But I also am one who decries the terrible waste of time and opportunity as children in some homes watch, hour upon hour, that which neither enlightens nor strengthens.

When I was a boy we lived in a large old house. One room was called the library. It had a solid table and a good lamp, three or four comfortable chairs with good light, and books in cases lining the walls. There were many volumes—the acquisitions of my father and mother over a period of many years. We were never forced to read those books, but they were placed where they were handy and where we could get at them whenever we wished. There was quiet in that room. It was understood that it was a place to study.

There were also magazines—the Church magazines and two or three other good magazines. There were books of history and literature, books on technical subjects, dictionaries, a multivolume encyclopedia, and an atlas of the world. There was no television, of course, at that time. Radio came along while I was growing up. But there was an environment of learning. I would not have you believe that we were great scholars. But we were exposed to great literature, great ideas from great thinkers, and the language of men and women who thought deeply and wrote beautifully.

In so many of our homes today there is not the possibility of such a library. Most families are cramped for space. But with planning there can be a corner, there can be an area that becomes something of a hideaway from the noises about us where one can sit and read and think. It is a wonderful thing to have a desk or a table, be it ever so simple, on which are found the standard works of the Church, a few good books, the magazines published by the Church, and other things worthy of our reading.

Begin early to expose children to books. The mother who fails to read to her small children does a disservice to them and a disservice to herself. It takes time, yes, much of it. It takes self-discipline. It takes organizing and budgeting the minutes and hours of the day. But it will never be a bore as you watch young minds come to know characters, expressions, and ideas. Good reading can become a love affair, far more fruitful in long-term effects than many other activities in which children use their time. It has been estimated that the average American child watches something like eight thousand hours of TV before he or she even starts school. A very large part of what the child watches is of questionable value.

Parents need to work at the matter of creating an atmosphere of learning in their homes. They need to let their children be exposed to great minds, great ideas, everlasting truth, and those things which will build and motivate for good.

The Lord has said to this people, "Seek ye out of the best books words of wisdom; seek learning, even by study and also by faith." (D&C 88:118.) I urge every parent within the sphere of my influence to try to create within your home an atmosphere of learning and the growth that will come of it.

THE DISCIPLINE OF LOVE

It is plainly evident that both the great good and the terrible evil found in the world today are the sweet and the bitter fruits of the rearing of yesterday's children. As we train a new generation, so will the world be in a few years. If you are worried about the future, then look today at the upbringing of children. In large measure the harshness that characterizes so much of our society is an outgrowth of the harshness imposed upon children years ago.

As boys and girls, we enjoyed the ward in which we lived. There were many kinds of people in that ward, and I think we knew them all. People seldom moved in those days. I think we loved all of them—all, that is, except one man. I must confess: I detested that man. I have since repented of that emotion, but as I look back I can sense again the intensity of my feeling. His young sons were our friends, but I regarded him as my enemy. Why this strong feeling? Because he had a vicious temper that flared at the slightest provocation, and he shouted at and cuffed his children in a manner I have never forgotten.

Perhaps I felt that way because of the home in which I grew, where there was a father who, by some quiet magic, was able to discipline his children without physical punishment, though occasionally they doubtless deserved it. I have seen the fruits of our neighbor's temper come alive in the troubled lives of his children.

I do not hesitate to say that no one who is a professed follower of Christ, and no one who is a professed member of Christ's Church, can engage in the abuse of children without offending God, who is their Father, and repudiating the teachings of the Savior and his prophets. It was Jesus himself who declared: "Whoso shall offend one of these little ones, . . . it were better for him that a millstone were hanged about his neck, and that he were drowned in the depth of the sea." (Matthew 18:6.)

Said Brigham Young: "Bring up your children in the love and fear of the Lord; study their dispositions and their temperaments, and deal with them accordingly, never allowing yourself to correct them in the heat of passion; teach them to love you rather than to fear you." (*Discourses of Brigham Young* [Salt Lake City: Deseret Book, 1941], p. 207.)

Discipline with severity or with cruelty inevitably leads not to correction but to resentment and bitterness. It cures nothing; it only aggravates the problem. It is self-defeating. The Lord, in setting forth the spirit of governance in his church, has also set forth the spirit of governance in the home in these great words of revelation: "No power or influence can or ought to be maintained, . . . only by persuasion, by long-suffering, by gentleness and meekness, and by love unfeigned; . . . reproving betimes with sharpness, when moved upon by the Holy Ghost; and then showing forth afterwards an increase of love toward him whom thou hast reproved, lest he esteem thee to be his enemy; that he may know that thy faithfulness is stronger than the cords of death." (D&C 121:41, **43-44.**)

Wrote Paul to the Ephesians: "And ye fathers, provoke not your children to wrath: but bring them up in the nurture and admonition of the Lord." (Ephesians 6:4.)

When little problems occur, as they inevitably will, restrain yourself. Call to mind the wisdom of the ancient proverb: "A soft answer turneth away wrath." (Proverbs 15:1.) There is no discipline in all the world like the discipline of love. It has a magic all its own.

THE PRACTICE OF PRAYER

Twice blessed is the child who, while he or she is so young as perhaps to be unable to comprehend the words, can nevertheless feel the spirit of prayer as a loving mother or a kind father helps with a few words of prayer at bedtime. Fortunate, indeed, are the boys and girls, including those in their teens, in whose homes there is the practice of morning and evening family prayer.

I know of no better way to develop a spirit of appreciation in children than for all of the members of the family to kneel to thank the Lord for his blessings. Such humble expression will do wonders to build within the hearts of children a recognition of the fact that God is the source of the precious gifts we have.

I know of no better way to cultivate a desire to do what is right than to humbly ask for forgiveness from him whose right it is to forgive, and to ask for strength to live above weakness.

What a wonderful thing it is to remember before the Lord those who are sick and in sorrow, those who are hungry and

71

destitute, those who are lonely and afraid, those who are in bondage and sore distress. When such prayers are uttered in sincerity, there will follow a greater desire to reach out to those in need. There will be increased respect and love for the bishop, for the stake president, for the President of the Church when they are remembered in the prayers of the family.

It is a significant thing to teach children how to pray concerning their own needs and righteous desires. As members of the family kneel together in supplication to the Almighty and speak with him of their needs, there will distill into the hearts of children a natural inclination in times of distress and extremity to turn to God as their Father and their friend. Let prayer, night and morning, as a family and as individuals, become a practice in which children grow while yet young. It will bless their lives forever. No parent in the Church can afford to neglect it.

I thank the Lord for the many good parents of the Church who are impressive examples of honesty and integrity before their children and before the world. I thank him for their faith and their faithfulness. I thank him for their great desire to nurture their children in light and truth as the Lord has commanded. May his blessings crown their efforts and may each someday be able to say, as said John of old, "I have no greater joy than to hear that my children walk in truth." (3 John 1:4.)

CHAPTER 11

THE
CONTINUING
PURSUIT OF TRUTH

There is incumbent upon each of us as members of The Church of Jesus Christ of Latter-day Saints the responsibility to observe the commandment to study and to learn. Said the Lord: "Seek ye out of the best books words of wisdom; seek learning, even by study and also by faith." (D&C 88:118.)

He further made it clear that our search for truth must be broad, that we are to learn "of things both in heaven and in the earth, and under the earth; things which have been, things which are, things which must shortly come to pass; things which are at home, things which are abroad; the wars and the perplexities of the nations, and the judgments which are on the land; and a knowledge also of countries and of kingdoms." (D&C 88:79.)

What a charge has been laid upon us to grow constantly toward eternity! None of us can assume that we have learned enough. As the door closes on one phase of life, it opens on another, where we must continue to pursue knowledge. Ours ought to be a ceaseless quest for truth. That truth must include spiritual and religious truth as well as secular. As we go forward with our lives and our search for truth, let us look for the good, the beautiful, the positive.

I try to read two or three newspapers a day. I sometimes read the columnists. I occasionally listen to commentators on television and radio. The writers are brilliant. They are men of incisive language, scintillating in expression. They are masters of the written word. But for the most part I find their attitude is negative. Regardless of whom they write about, they seem to look for failings and weaknesses. They are constantly criticizing, seldom praising.

And this spirit is not limited to the columnists and commentators. Read the letters to the editor. Some of them are filled with venom, written by persons who seem to find no good in the world or in their associates. Criticism, faultfinding, evil speaking—these are of the spirit of our day. From many directions we are told that nowhere is there a person of integrity holding political office. People in business are crooks. Utilities are out to rob you. Everywhere is heard the snide remark, the sarcastic gibe, the cutting down of associates. Sadly, these are too often the essence of our conversation. In our homes, wives weep and children give up under the barrage of criticism leveled by husbands and fathers. Criticism is the forerunner of divorce, the cultivator of rebellion, sometimes a catalyst that leads to failure. In the Church it sows the seed of inactivity and finally apostasy.

I am asking that we stop seeking out the storms and enjoy more fully the sunlight. I am suggesting that as we go through life we "accentuate the positive." I am asking that we look a little deeper for the good, that we still voices of insult and sarcasm, that we more generously compliment virtue and effort. I am not asking that all criticism be silenced. Growth comes of correction. Strength comes of repentance. Wise are those who can acknowledge mistakes pointed out by others and change their course.

What I am suggesting is that each of us turn from the negativism that so permeates our society and look for the remarkable good among those with whom we associate, that we speak of one another's virtues more than we speak of one another's faults, that optimism replace pessimism, that our faith exceed our fears. When I was a young man and was prone

74

to speak critically, my father would say, "Cynics do not contribute, skeptics do not create, doubters do not achieve."

Looking at the dark side of things always leads to a spirit of pessimism, which so often leads to defeat. If ever there was a man who rallied a nation in its time of deepest distress, it was Winston Churchill. Bombs were then falling on London. The Nazi war machine had overrun Austria, Czechoslovakia, France, Belgium, Holland, and Norway, and was moving into Russia. Most of Europe was in the grasp of tyranny, and England was to be next. In that dangerous hour, when the hearts of many were failing, Churchill spoke: "Do not let us speak of darker days; let us speak rather of sterner days. These are not dark days; these are great days—the greatest days our country has ever lived; and we must all thank God that we have been allowed, each of us according to our stations, to play a part in making these days memorable in the history of our race." (Address at Harrow School, October 29, 1941.)

Following the terrible catastrophe at Dunkirk, many prophets of doom foretold the end of Britain. But in that dark and solemn hour this remarkable man said, and I heard him say these words as they were broadcast across America, "We shall not flag or fail. . . . We shall fight in France, we shall fight on the seas and oceans, we shall fight with growing confidence and growing strength in the air, we shall defend our island, whatever the cost may be, we shall fight on the beaches, we shall fight on the landing grounds, we shall fight in the fields and in the streets, we shall fight in the hills; we shall never surrender." (Speech on Dunkirk, House of Commons, June 4, 1940.)

It was this kind of talk, which saw victory distantly through the dark clouds of war, and not the critical faultfinding of cynics, that preserved the people of Britain and saved that nation from catastrophe.

I have little doubt that many of us are troubled with fears concerning ourselves. We are in a period of stress across the world. There are occasionally hard days for each of us. Do not despair. Do not give up. Look for the sunlight through the clouds. Opportunities will eventually open to you. Do not let the prophets of gloom endanger your possibilities.

This counsel also relates to us as members of the Lord's Church. We seem to have a host of critics. Some appear intent on trying to destroy us. They mock that which is sacred. They belittle that which we call divine. Some have said that we are trapped by our history; others have worked with great diligence seeking flaws in our early leaders. We are accused of being opposed to reason and rational thought.

These are serious accusations against a church that teaches that "the glory of God is intelligence, or, in other words, light and truth." (D&C 93:36.) These are serious charges against a church that each year spends millions of dollars of its resources on the education of its youth. Those who criticize us have lost sight of the glory and wonder of this work. In their cultivated faultfinding, they do not see the majesty of the great onrolling of this cause. They have lost sight of the spark that was kindled in Palmyra and which is now lighting fires of faith across the earth in many lands and in many languages. Wearing the spectacles of humanism, they fail to realize that spiritual emotions, with recognition of the influence of the Holy Spirit, had as much to do with the actions of our forebears as did the processes of the mind. They have failed to realize that religion is as much concerned with the heart as it is with the intellect.

George Santayana once said:

> O World, thou choosest not the better part!
> It is not wisdom to be only wise,
> And on the inward vision close the eyes,
> But it is wisdom to believe the heart.

We have critics who appear to cull out of a vast panorama of information those items which demean and belittle some men and women of the past who worked so hard in laying the foundation of this great cause. They find readers of their

76

works who seem to delight in picking up these tidbits, in chewing them over and relishing them. In so doing they are savoring some small morsel, rather than eating a beautiful and satisfying dinner of many courses.

My plea is that as we continue our search for truth, particularly we who are members of the Church, we look for strength and goodness rather than weakness and foibles in those who did so great a work in their time. We recognize that our forebears were human. They doubtless made mistakes. Some of them acknowledged making mistakes. But the mistakes were minor when compared with the marvelous work they accomplished. To highlight mistakes and gloss over the greater good is to draw a caricature. Caricatures are amusing, but they are often ugly and dishonest. A man may have a wart on his cheek and still have a face of beauty and strength, but if the wart is emphasized unduly in relation to his other features, the portrait is lacking in integrity.

There was only one perfect man who ever walked the earth. The Lord has used imperfect people in the process of building his perfect society. If some of them have occasionally stumbled, or if their characters may have been slightly flawed in one way or another, the wonder is the greater that they have accomplished so much.

I mention these things because I hope that we will cultivate an attitude of looking for positive elements that lead to growth and enthusiasm. We are not trapped by our history. That history contains the foundation of this work. It sets forth in some detail the circumstances and the events connected with the restoration of the gospel of Jesus Christ. If the picture is not always complete, or if there are various versions differing somewhat concerning certain events, intellectual honesty would point out that there is nothing new in this. For instance, the New Testament includes four Gospels. The tone of each is the same, but the various writers made particular choices of what they wished to emphasize, and only by reading them all and harmonizing them do we get the fullest possible picture of the Son of God, who walked the roads of Palestine.

I do not fear truth. I welcome it. But I wish all of my facts to be in their proper context, with emphasis on those elements which explain the great growth and power of this organization. I have felt the need to say these things because there are those today who are emphasizing the negative and who seem to miss entirely the great inspiration of this work.

This leads me to say a few words on intellectualism. A scholar once expressed the view that the Church is an enemy of intellectualism. If he meant by intellectualism that branch of philosophy which teaches "the doctrine that knowledge is wholly or chiefly derived from pure reason" and that "reason is the final principle of reality," then, yes, we are opposed to so narrow an interpretation as applicable to religion. (Quotations from the *Random House Dictionary of the English Language,* p. 738.) Such an interpretation excludes the power of the Holy Spirit in speaking to and through men.

Of course we believe in the cultivation of the mind, but the intellect is not the only source of knowledge. There is a promise, given under inspiration from the Almighty, set forth in these beautiful words: "God shall give unto you knowledge by his Holy Spirit, yea, by the unspeakable gift of the Holy Ghost." (D&C 121:26.)

The humanists who criticize the Lord's work, the so-called intellectualists who demean, speak only from ignorance of spiritual manifestation. They have not heard the voice of the Spirit. They have not heard it because they have not sought after it and prepared themselves to be worthy of it. Then, supposing that knowledge comes only of reasoning and of the workings of the mind, they deny that which comes by the power of the Holy Ghost.

The things of God are understood by the Spirit of God. That Spirit is real. To those who have experienced its workings, the knowledge so gained is as real as that which is acquired through the operation of the five senses. I testify of this. And

I am confident that most members of the Church can so testify. I urge each of us to continue to cultivate a heart in tune with the Spirit. If we will do so, our lives will be enriched. We will feel a kinship with God our Eternal Father. We will taste a sweetness of joy that can be had in no other way.

Let us not be trapped by the sophistries of the world, which for the most part are negative and which so often bear sour fruit. Let us walk with faith in the future, speaking affirmatively and cultivating an attitude of confidence. As we do so, our strength will give strength to others.

On one occasion when the Savior was walking among a crowd, a woman who had long been sick touched his garment. He perceived that strength had gone out of him. The strength that was his had strengthened her. So it may be with each of us.

Said the Lord to Peter: "Simon, Simon, behold, Satan hath desired to have you, that he may sift you as wheat: but I have prayed for thee, that thy faith fail not: and when thou art converted, strengthen thy brethren." (Luke 22:31-32.)

Let us not partake of the negative spirit so rife in our times. There is so much of the sweet and the decent and the beautiful to build upon. We are partakers of the gospel of Jesus Christ. The gospel means "good news." The message of the Lord is one of hope and salvation. The voice of the Lord is a voice of glad tidings. The work of the Lord is a work of glorious accomplishment.

In a dark and troubled hour the Lord said to those he loved, "Let not your heart be troubled, neither let it be afraid." (John 14:27.) These great words of confidence are a beacon to each of us. In him we may indeed have trust, for he and his promises will never fail.

CHAPTER 12

"WITH ALL THY GETTING GET UNDERSTANDING"

I remember a day some years ago when I strolled about the campus of one of our universities. I was impressed with the splendor of the buildings, the immaculate laboratories, the teaching theaters, the magnificent library, the dormitories, the gymnasiums. But I was even more impressed with the students. There were thousands of them — handsome young men and beautiful young women, seemingly serious and intent and earnest.

I am awed by the great forces of knowledge represented in our time. Never before have so many been educated in the learning of the world. What a powerful thing it is — the intensive schooling of a large percentage of the youth of the world, who meet daily at the feet of instructors to garner knowledge from all the ages of man. The extent of that knowledge is staggering. It encompasses the stars of the universe, the geology of the earth, the history of nations, the culture and language of peoples, the operation of governments, the laws of commerce, the behavior of the atom, the functions of the body, and the wonders of the mind.

With so much knowledge available, one would think that the world might well be near a state of perfection. Yet we are constantly made aware of the other side of the coin — of the sickness of society, of the contentions and troubles that bring misery into the lives of millions. Each day we are made increasingly aware of the fact that life is more than science and mathematics, more than history and literature. There is need for another education, without which the substance of secular learning may lead only to destruction. I refer to the education of the heart, of the conscience, of the character, of the spirit— those indefinable aspects of our personalities which determine so certainly what we are and what we do in our relationships one with another.

Over fifty years ago while serving in England as a missionary, I went to the London Central YMCA. I suppose that old building has long since gone, but I will never forget the words that visitors saw in the foyer each time they entered. They were the words of Solomon: "With all thy getting get understanding." (Proverbs 4:7.)

Understanding of what? Understanding of ourselves, of the purposes of life, of our relationship to God who is our Father, of the great divinely given principles that for centuries have provided the sinew of man's real progress!

I cannot discuss all of these great principles, but I desire to suggest three: gratitude, virtue, and faith. I offer them in a spirit of invitation. Let these principles be added to our vast store of secular knowledge to become cornerstones on which all of us may establish lives that will be fruitful, productive, and happy. I believe they are fundamental to the full development of every child of God.

GRATITUDE

Gratitude is a divine principle. The Lord has declared through revelation: "Thou shalt thank the Lord thy God in all things. . . . And in nothing doth man offend God, or against none is his wrath kindled, save those who confess not his hand in all things." (D&C 59:7, 21.)

Our society is afflicted by a spirit of thoughtless arrogance unbecoming to those who have been so magnificently blessed.

How grateful we should be for the bounties we enjoy. Absence of gratitude is the mark of the narrow, uneducated mind. It bespeaks a lack of knowledge and the ignorance of self-sufficiency. It expresses itself in ugly egotism and frequently in wanton mischief. We have seen our beaches, our parks, our forests littered with ugly refuse by those who evidently have no appreciation for nature's beauty. I have driven through thousands of acres of blackened land scourged by a fire evidently set by a careless smoker whose only concern had been the selfish pleasure gained from a cigarette.

Where there is appreciation, there is courtesy; there is concern for the rights and property of others. Without appreciation, there is arrogance and evil. Where there is gratitude, there is humility, as opposed to pride.

How magnificently we are blessed! How thankful we ought to be! A bulletin of some years ago of the Royal Bank of Canada dealt with underprivileged people of the world: "It is difficult for [most] North Americans to understand the plight of people in underdeveloped countries, because [most of us] have never been hungry. No one dies here of starvation. Elsewhere more than 1,500 million people go to bed hungry every night. . . . The fact is that not more than one in a hundred of the people in underdeveloped countries will ever, in all his life, have what a North American family would consider a good, square meal."

Let us cultivate a spirit of thanksgiving for the blessing of life and for the marvelous gifts and privileges each of us enjoys. The Lord has said that the meek shall inherit the earth. (Matthew 5:5.) I cannot escape the interpretation that meekness implies a spirit of gratitude as opposed to an attitude of self-sufficiency, an acknowledgment of a greater power beyond oneself, a recognition of God, and an acceptance of his commandments. This is the beginning of wisdom. Walk with gratitude before him who is the giver of life and every good gift.

VIRTUE

Associated with gratitude is virtue. I think they are related because he who is disposed to shun virtue lacks appreciation of life, its purposes, and the happiness and well-being of others.

An observer of our plight has written the following: "We are witnessing the death of the old morality. The established moral guidelines have been yanked from our hands. . . . We are left floundering, in a money-motivated, sex-obsessed, big-city dominated society. We must figure out for ourselves how to apply the traditional moral principles to the problems of our times. Many find this burden too heavy." (*Look,* September 1963, p. 74.)

Challenging though it may be, there is a way to apply traditional moral principles in our day. For some unknown reason, there is constantly appearing the false rationalization that at one time in the long-ago, virtue was easy and that now it is difficult. I would like to remind any who feel that way that there has never been a time since the Creation when the same forces were not at work that are at work today. The proposal made by Potiphar's wife to Joseph in Egypt is no different from that faced by many people in our day.

The influences today may be more apparent and more seductive, but they are no more compelling. We cannot be shielded entirely from these influences. They are all about us. Our culture is saturated with them. But the same kind of self-discipline exercised by Joseph will yield the same beneficial result. Notwithstanding the so-called "new morality," notwithstanding the much-discussed changes in moral standards, there is no adequate substitute for virtue. God's standards may be challenged everywhere throughout the world, but God has not abrogated his commandments.

The violation of his commandments in this age, as in any other, brings only regret, sorrow, loss of self-respect, and in many cases tragedy. Rationalization and equivocation will not erase the cankering scar that blights the self-respect of a person who disobeys the law of chastity. Self-justification will never mend the heart of a person who has drifted into moral tragedy.

In April 1942, the First Presidency of the Church issued a message that has the tone of scripture: "To the youth of the Church . . . above all we plead with you to live clean, for the unclean life leads only to suffering, misery, and woe physically—and spiritually it is the path to destruction. How glorious and near to the angels is youth that is clean; this youth has joy unspeakable here and eternal happiness hereafter." (*Improvement Era* 45:273.)

It is verily true, as the scriptures state: "The commandment is a lamp; and the law is light." (Proverbs 6:23.) Do not mock God. Do not flout his law. Let virtue be a cornerstone on which to build your life.

FAITH

When I discuss faith, I do not mean it in an abstract sense. I mean it as a living, vital force with recognition of God as our Father and Jesus Christ as our Savior. When we accept this basic premise, there will come an acceptance of their teachings and an obedience that will bring peace and joy in this life and exaltation in the life to come.

Faith is not a theological platitude. It is a fact of life. Faith can become the very wellspring of purposeful living. There is no more compelling motivation to worthwhile endeavor than the knowledge that we are children of God, the Creator of the universe, our all-wise Heavenly Father! God expects us to do something with our lives, and he will give us help when help is sought.

Jesus said: "Learn of me. . . . For my yoke is easy, and my burden is light." (Matthew 11:29-30.) I should like to suggest that we follow that injunction given by the Son of God. With all of our learning, let us also learn of him. With all of our study, we need to seek knowledge of the Master. That knowledge will complement in a wonderful way our secular training

84

and will give us character and a fulness of life that can come in no other way.

We were aboard a plane some years ago flying between Honolulu and Los Angeles. It was in the days when only propeller-driven aircraft were available. About midway in the journey one of the motors stopped. There was a decrease in speed, a lowering in altitude, and a certain amount of nervousness among those aboard. The fact of the matter was that much of the power was missing, and the hazards were increased accordingly. Without that power, we could not fly high, fast, and safely.

It is so with our lives when we discount the need for faith and disregard knowledge of the Lord. Passive acceptance of the Lord is not enough. Vibrant testimony comes of anxious seeking. Strength comes of active service in the Master's cause. "Learn of me," was Jesus' injunction. He further declared that he who does the will of the Father "shall know of the doctrine, whether it be of God, or whether I speak of myself." (John 7:17.)

And so, while we read math and physics and chemistry, we need to read also the Gospels of the New Testament and the testament of the New World, the Book of Mormon.

I cherish the words of Paul—he who had traveled far and suffered much and grown ripe in wisdom. These words were written to Timothy while Paul was a prisoner of Nero in Rome: "God hath not given us the spirit of fear; but of power, and of love, and of a sound mind. Be not thou therefore ashamed of the testimony of our Lord." (2 Timothy 1:7-8.) To every Latter-day Saint I commend this stirring injunction. This is the spirit that will reform the world.

I recall the statement of Charles Malik: "In this fearful age it is not enough to be happy and prosperous and secure yourselves. . . . You must have a message to proclaim to others; you must mean something in terms of ideas and attitudes and fundamental outlook on life; and this something must vibrate with relevance to all conditions of men."

Let us take upon ourselves the name of the Lord and then with faith go forth to share with relevance that which will affect the lives of mankind and bring peace and joy to the world. The world needs a generation of men and women of learning and influence who can and will stand up and in sincerity and without equivocation declare that God lives and that Jesus is the Christ. As we pursue our secular studies, let us also add to our lives the cultivation of the Spirit. If we do so, God will bless us with that peace and those blessings which come from him alone.

CHAPTER 13

SMALL ACTS
LEAD TO GREAT
CONSEQUENCES

Have you ever noticed a large gate in a farm fence? As you open it or close it, there appears to be very little movement at the hinge. But there is great movement at the perimeter.

Speaking to the Prophet Joseph Smith in 1831, the Lord said: "Out of small things proceedeth that which is great." (D&C 64:33.) It is so with good or evil. Small, kind acts can grow into mammoth, good institutions. It is so likewise with evil things. Small acts of dishonesty, small acts of an immoral nature, small outbursts of anger can grow into great and terrible tragedies.

There stood once on Temple Square in Salt Lake City a bowery—a rather crude structure in which the Saints met in those days of their poverty. In September 1857, there was presented in that old bowery on a Sunday afternoon what was really the concluding act of a drama of great tragedy.

On that Sunday Brigham Young was conducting a meeting and introduced to the congregation a man who appeared to be old and infirm and weary of life. Said President Brigham Young to the congregation:

"Brother Thomas B. Marsh, formerly the President of the Quorum of the Twelve Apostles, has now come to us, after an absence of nearly nineteen years. He is on the stand to-day, and wishes to make a few remarks to the congregation. . . . He

87

came into my office and wished to know . . . whether there could be a reconciliation between himself and the Church of the living God. He reflected for a moment and said, I am reconciled to the Church, but I want to know whether the Church can be reconciled to me." Then President Young explained, "He is here, and I want him to say what he may wish to. Brethren and sisters, I now introduce to you brother Thomas B. Marsh. When the Quorum of the Twelve was first organized, he was appointed to be their President."

Brother Marsh then rose to the pulpit. This man, who was named the first president of the Council of the Twelve Apostles and to whom the Lord had spoken in so marvelous a manner, as recorded in section 112 of the Doctrine and Covenants, said to the people:

"I do not know that I can make all this vast congregation hear and understand me. My voice never was very strong, but it has been very much weakened of late years by the afflicting rod of Jehovah. He loved me too much to let me go without whipping. I have seen the hand of the Lord in the chastisement which I have received. I have seen and known that it has proved he loved me; for if he had not cared anything about me, he would not have taken me by the arm and given me such a shaking.

"If there are any among this people who should ever apostatize and do as I have done, prepare your backs for a good whipping, if you are such as the Lord loves. But if you will take my advice, you will stand by the authorities; but if you go away and the Lord loves you as much as he did me, he will whip you back again.

"Many have said to me, 'How is it that a man like you, who understood so much of the revelations of God as recorded in the Book of Doctrine and Covenants, should fall away?' I told them not to feel too secure, but to take heed lest they also should fall; for I had no scruples in my mind as to the possibility of men falling away.

"I can say, in reference to the Quorum of the Twelve, to

88

which I belonged, that I did not consider myself a whit behind any of them, and I suppose that others had the same opinion; but, let no one feel too secure; for, before you think of it, your steps will slide. You will not then think nor feel for a moment as you did before you lost the Spirit of Christ; for when men apostatize, they are left to grovel in the dark." (*Journal of Discourses* 5:206.)

Speaking in a voice that was difficult to hear, and appearing as an old man when he was actually only fifty-seven years of age, the former apostle spoke of the travails through which he had passed before he had finally made his way to the valley of the Great Salt Lake and asked that he might be baptized again into the Church.

I wondered, as I read that story so filled with pathos, what had brought him to this sorry state. I discovered it, in the *Journal of Discourses,* in a talk to the Saints in this same bowery the year before by George A. Smith. I think it is worth the telling to illustrate to all of us the need to be careful in dealing with small matters that can lead to great consequences.

According to the account by Elder Smith, while the Saints were in Far West, Missouri, "the wife of Thomas B. Marsh, who was then President of the Twelve Apostles, and Sister Harris concluded they would exchange milk, in order to make a little larger cheese than they otherwise could. To be sure to have justice done, it was agreed that they should not save the strippings, but that the milk and strippings should all go together." Now for you who have never been around a cow, I should say that the strippings come at the end of the milking and are richer in cream.

"Mrs. Harris, it appeared, was faithful to the agreement and carried to Mrs. Marsh the milk and strippings, but Mrs. Marsh, wishing to make some extra good cheese, saved a pint of strippings from each cow and sent Mrs. Harris the milk without the strippings."

A quarrel arose, and the matter was referred to the home teachers. They found Mrs. Marsh guilty of failure to keep her agreement. She and her husband were upset, and "an appeal was taken from the teacher to the bishop, and a regular Church trial was had. President Marsh did not consider that the bishop had done him and his lady justice, for they [that is, the bishop's court] decided that the strippings were wrongfully saved, and that the woman had violated her covenant.

"Marsh immediately took an appeal to the High Council, who investigated the question with much patience, and," said George A. Smith, "I assure you they were a grave body. Marsh being extremely anxious to maintain the character of his wife, . . . made a desperate defence, but the High Council finally confirmed the bishop's decision.

"Marsh, not being satisfied, took an appeal to the First Presidency of the Church, and Joseph and his counselors had to sit upon the case, and they approved the decision of the high council.

"This little affair," Brother Smith continued, "kicked up a considerable breeze, and Thomas B. Marsh then declared that he would sustain the character of his wife, even if he had to go to hell for it.

"The then President of the Twelve Apostles, the man who should have been the first to do justice and cause reparation to be made for wrong, committed by any member of his family, took that position, and what next? He went before a magistrate and swore that the 'Mormons' were hostile towards the State of Missouri.

"That affidavit brought from the government of Missouri an exterminating order, which drove some 15,000 Saints from their homes and habitations, and some thousands perished through suffering the exposure consequent on this state of affairs." (*Journal of Discourses* 3:283-84.)

What a very small and trivial thing—a little cream over which two women quarreled. But it led to, or at least was a factor in, Governor Boggs's cruel exterminating order that drove the Saints from the state of Missouri, with all of the terrible suffering and consequent death that followed. The man who should have settled this little quarrel but who, rather, pursued it, troubling the officers of the Church right up to the Presidency, literally went through hell for it. He lost his standing in the Church. He lost his testimony of the gospel. For nineteen years he walked in poverty and darkness and bitterness, experiencing illness and loneliness. He grew old before his time. Finally, like the prodigal son in the parable of the Savior, he recognized his foolishness and painfully made his way to the Salt Lake Valley, where he asked Brigham Young to forgive him and permit his rebaptism into the Church. He had been the first President of the Council of the Twelve, loved, respected, and honored in the days of Kirtland and the early days of Far West. Now he asked only that he might be ordained a deacon and become a doorkeeper in the house of the Lord.

We have all seen cases somewhat similar in our own time. It is so easy to stumble. It is sometimes so hard to keep our voices low when small things provoke us. May we resolve in our hearts to live the gospel, to be faithful and true, to have the strength to look above small things that could lead to argument and trouble, to be forgiving one of another, to "look to God and live." (Alma 37:47.)

Let us remember always that we are sons and daughters of God, children born with a divine birthright, partakers of the glorious gospel of Jesus Christ, the beneficiaries of the priesthood restored by the Almighty for the blessing of his sons and daughters. Let us walk with integrity and honesty in all of our dealings one with another. Let us subdue any arrogance or pride and walk humbly before God, with appreciation and respect for all with whom we associate.

CHAPTER 14

"PRAISE TO THE MAN"

Many years ago when at the age of twelve I was ordained a deacon, my father, who was president of our stake, took me to my first stake priesthood meeting. In those days these meetings were held on a week night. I recall that we went to the Tenth Ward building in Salt Lake City. He walked up to the stand and I sat on the back row, feeling a little alone and uncomfortable in that hall filled with strong men who had been ordained to the priesthood of God. The meeting was called to order, the opening song was announced, and, as was then the custom, we all stood to sing. There were perhaps as many as four hundred there. Together these men lifted their strong voices, some with the accents of the European lands from which they had come as converts, all singing these words with a great spirit of conviction and testimony:

> *Praise to the man who communed with Jehovah!*
> *Jesus anointed that Prophet and Seer.*
> *Blessed to open the last dispensation,*
> *Kings shall extol him, and nations revere.*
> —*Hymns,* 1985, no. 27

They were singing of the Prophet Joseph Smith, and as they did so, there came into my heart a great surge of love for and belief in the mighty Prophet of this dispensation. In my childhood I had been taught much about him in meetings and classes in our ward as well as in our home, but my experience in that stake priesthood meeting was different. I knew then, by the power of the Holy Ghost, that Joseph Smith was indeed a prophet of God.

It is true that during the years that followed there were times when that testimony wavered somewhat, particularly in the seasons of my undergraduate university work. However, that conviction never left me entirely; and it has grown stronger through the years, partly because of the challenges of those days that compelled me to read and study and make certain for myself. President Harold B. Lee once said that our testimonies need renewing every day. In harmony with that principle, I desire to strengthen our testimonies of the great work that the God of heaven has permitted to transpire in these last days.

A few years ago, I received a letter written by an evangelist who with diatribe lashed out against the Prophet Joseph Smith, calling him a wicked imposter, a fraud, a fake, and a deceiver, and declaring that he was undertaking a campaign to spread his own views. Whatever became of his work, I do not know. It would not have been significant. That kind of work may topple a few of the weak, but it only strengthens the strong. And long after that man and others of his kind have gone down to silence, the name of Joseph Smith will continue to ring with honor and love in the hearts of an ever-growing band of Latter-day Saints in an ever-increasing number of nations.

I remember being in Nauvoo, the City of Joseph, with two brethren of the First Quorum of the Seventy and twelve mission presidents and their wives for a mission presidents' seminar. The touch of autumn was on the land—the leaves golden, a little haze in the air, the nights cool, the days warm. The tourist season was over, and the city was peaceful and beautiful.

We held our first meeting in the restored Seventies Hall,

where in the 1840s men prepared themselves, through study and through teaching one another the doctrine of the kingdom, to go out to declare the message of the gospel to the world. The work that went on there was a forerunner of the missionary training centers of the Church. As we met in that and other homes and halls in Nauvoo, in our minds and hearts it was as if the figures of the past were with us—Joseph and Hyrum, Brigham Young, Heber C. Kimball, John Taylor, Wilford Woodruff, the brothers Pratt—Orson and Parley—and a host of others.

This was indeed Joseph's city. He was the prophet who planned it, and his followers had built it. It became the largest and the most impressive city in the state of Illinois. With sturdy brick homes; with halls for worship, instruction, and entertainment; and with the magnificent temple standing on the crest of the slope up from the river, this community on the Mississippi was put together as if its builders were to be there for a century or more.

There, before that tragic day at Carthage, the Prophet was at the zenith of his mortal career. As I stood where he once stood and gazed on the city, I thought of the events that had brought him there, reviewing in my mind his inheritance.

I thought of his forebears who generations before had left the British Isles and come to Boston; of their lives in the New World, through five generations on his father's side and four on his mother's; of their labors in clearing land in Massachusetts, New Hampshire, and Vermont to build farms and homes; of their distinguished service in the war for independence; of the adversities and the failures they experienced in trying to wrest a living from the granite hills among which they lived. I thought of the little boy, born in Sharon in December 1805, given his father's name. I reflected on that terrifying period of sickness when typhus fever struck the family, and osteomyelitis, with great pain and debilitating infection, settled in Joseph's leg. That was while the family lived in Lebanon, New Hampshire; and how remarkable it was that only a few miles away, at the academy in Hanover, was Dr. Nathan Smith, who had developed a procedure by which that infected leg might be saved.

But the cure was not to be accomplished without terrible suffering. In fact, today it is difficult to conceive how the little boy stood it as his father held him in his arms and his mother walked and prayed among the trees of the farm to escape his screams while the surgeon made the long incision and with forceps broke off the portions of infected bone without benefit of any kind of anesthesia. Perhaps remembrance of that intense suffering helped prepare Joseph Smith for the later tarring and feathering at Hiram, Ohio; the foul jail at Liberty, Missouri; and the shots of the mob at Carthage, Illinois.

As I contemplated Joseph Smith's life, I thought of the forces that moved the Smith family from generations of life in New England to western New York, where they had to come if the foreordained purposes of God were to be accomplished. I thought of the loss of the family farm, of poor crops in that thin soil, of the great freeze of 1816 when a killing frost in July forced upon them the decision to look elsewhere; then of the move to Palmyra, of the purchase of a farm in Manchester, and of the revivalist preachers who stirred the people and so confused the young boy that he determined to ask God for wisdom.

That was the real beginning of it all, that spring day in the year 1820 when he knelt among the trees, opened his mouth in prayer, and beheld a glorious vision in which he spoke with God, the Eternal Father, and his Son, the risen Lord Jesus Christ. Then followed the years of instruction, the instructor an angel of God who on a dozen and more occasions taught, rebuked, warned, and comforted the boy as he grew into a young man.

And so, while in Nauvoo I reflected on the preparation for prophethood; I reflected on this amazing Joseph Smith. I cannot expect his detractors to know of his prophetic calling by the power of the Holy Ghost, but I can raise some questions for them to deal with before they can dismiss Joseph Smith. I raise only three of many questions that might be asked: First, what do you do with the Book of Mormon? Second, how do you explain Joseph's power to influence strong men to follow him, even unto death? And third, how do you rationalize the fulfillment of his prophecies?

First, what do we do with the Book of Mormon? I take in my hand a copy of the book. I read its words. I have read Joseph Smith's explanation of how it came to be. To the unbelieving it is a story difficult to accept, and critics for generations have worn out their lives writing books intended to refute that story and to offer other explanations than the one given by Joseph the Prophet. But to the open-minded, this critical writing has only stimulated them to dig deeper; and the more deeply they dig, the greater the accumulation of evidence for the validity of Joseph Smith's story. Still, as has been demonstrated for a hundred and fifty years, the truth of the Book of Mormon will not be determined by literary analysis or by scientific research, although these continue to be reassuring. The truth about the origins of the Book of Mormon will be determined today and tomorrow, as it has been throughout the yesterdays, by reading the book in a spirit of reverence and respect and prayer.

Some time ago, I received a letter from a father who said that, in response to a challenge I once offered at general conference that we read the Book of Mormon, he and his family were going to read the first edition, which touched so deeply many strong and able men who read it when it first came from the press. I commended him but hastened to add that no one need look for a first edition to get the spirit of this remarkable volume. Every one of the more than a million copies that will be printed this year carries that same spirit, includes that same marvelous promise, and will yield the same result in testimony concerning the truth of the book.

The Book of Mormon is here to be handled and to be read with prayer and earnest inquiry. All the work of its critics since its publication has lacked credibility and has been without effect on those who have prayerfully read the book and received by the power of the Holy Ghost a witness of its truth. If there were no other evidence for the divine mission of Joseph Smith, the Book of Mormon would stand as an irrefutable witness of that fact. To think that anyone, less than one inspired, could bring forth a volume that would have so profound an effect for good upon so many others is to imagine that which simply cannot be. The evidence for the truth of the Book of Mormon is found in the lives of the millions who have read it, prayed about it, and received a witness of its truth.

My second question, how do you explain Joseph Smith's power to influence strong men and women to follow him, even unto death, is similarly difficult to dismiss. Anyone who has any doubt about Joseph Smith's powers of leadership need only look at those who were attracted to him. They did not come for wealth. They did not come for political power. They were not drawn by dreams of military conquest. His offering to them was none of these; rather, it concerned only salvation through faith in the Lord Jesus Christ. It involved persecution with its pain and losses, long and lonely missions, separation from family and friends, and in many cases death itself.

Take, for instance, Orson Hyde. He was a clerk in the village of Kirtland when he met Joseph Smith. It was to this unknown, unpromising young seller of buttons and thread and calico that Joseph, speaking in the name of the Lord, said that he (Orson Hyde) was ordained "to proclaim the everlasting gospel, by the Spirit of the living God, from people to people, and from land to land, in the congregations of the wicked, in their synagogues, reasoning with and expounding all scriptures unto them." (D&C 68:1.) This young man, under the inspiration of that prophetic call, walked two thousand miles on foot through Rhode Island, Massachusetts, Maine, and New York, "reasoning with and expounding all scriptures" unto all whom he met.

I recall visiting Orson Hyde's home in Nauvoo, the comfortable home he left to travel to England and Germany and to visit Constantinople, Cairo, and Alexandria en route to Jerusalem, where on October 24, 1841, he stood on the Mount of Olives and dedicated by the authority of the holy priesthood the land of Palestine for the return of the Jews. That was a quarter of a century before Herzl undertook the work of gathering the Jews to their homeland.

For another example, take Willard Richards, an educated man who, when Joseph and Hyrum Smith surrendered to the governor of Illinois and were placed in Carthage Jail, was among a handful of men who went with them. By the afternoon of June 27, 1844, most had been sent to take care of certain matters of business, leaving only John Taylor and Willard Richards with the Prophet and his brother. That afternoon following dinner, the jailer, knowing that a mob had gathered outside, suggested that the prisoners would be safer in the cell of the jail. Turning to Willard Richards, Joseph asked, "If we go into the cell will you go with us?"

To this Elder Richards responded: "Brother Joseph, you did not ask me to cross the river with you . . . you did not ask me to come to Carthage . . . you did not ask me to come to jail with you—and do you think I would forsake you now? But I will tell you what I will do; if you are condemned to be hung for 'treason,' I will be hung in your stead, and you shall go free." (B. H. Roberts, *A Comprehensive History of the Church* 2:283.)

Strong and intelligent men do not demonstrate that kind of love for a charlatan or a fraud. That kind of love comes of God and the recognition of integrity in individuals. It is an expression of the spirit and reflects the example of the Savior, who gave his life for all men and who declared, "Greater love hath no man than this, that a man lay down his life for his friends." (John 15:13.)

There were so many others—the Youngs, the Kimballs, the Taylors, the Snows, the Pratts, and more upon more—who when they first met Joseph Smith seemed ordinary and

98

unpromising, but who under the power of the truths and priesthood that Joseph Smith restored became giants in achievement through their service to others.

Finally, what of Joseph Smith's prophecies? There were more than a few, and they were fulfilled. Among the most notable was the revelation on the Civil War. You are familiar with it; it was spoken on Christmas Day, 1832. There were many high-minded men and women who deplored the institution of slavery then common in the South, and there was much talk of abolition. Who but a prophet of God would have dared to say, twenty-nine years before it was to happen, that "war [would] be poured out upon all nations," beginning "at the rebellion of South Carolina," and that "the Southern States [would] be divided against the Northern States"? (D&C 87:1-3.) This remarkable prediction saw its fulfillment with the firing on Fort Sumter in Charleston Harbor in 1861. How could Joseph Smith have possibly foreseen with such accuracy an event that would come twenty-nine years after he spoke of it? Only by the spirit of prophecy that was in him.

Or again, consider the equally remarkable prophecy concerning the movement of the Saints to the mountain valleys. The Saints were then living in Nauvoo and its sister community across the Mississippi in Iowa and were enjoying a prosperity they had not previously known. They were building a temple and other substantial structures. Their new homes were of brick, constructed to endure. And yet one day in August 1842, while visiting in Montrose, Joseph prophesied "that the Saints would continue to suffer much affliction and would be driven to the Rocky Mountains, many would apostatize, others would be put to death by [their] persecutors or lose their lives in consequence of exposure or disease, and [speaking to those who were present] some of you will live to go and assist in making settlements and build cities and see the Saints become a mighty people in the midst of the Rocky Mountains." (*History of the Church* 5:85.)

Viewed in the context of the time and circumstances, this

statement is nothing less than remarkable. Only a man speaking with a knowledge beyond his own could have uttered words that would be so literally fulfilled.

And what of this prophecy, which so magnificently foresaw the joyous destiny of this church?

"Our missionaries are going forth to different nations . . . the Standard of Truth has been erected; no unhallowed hand can stop the work from progressing; persecutions may rage, mobs may combine, armies may assemble, calumny may defame, but the truth of God will go forth boldly, nobly, and independent, till it has penetrated every continent, visited every clime, swept every country, and sounded in every ear, till the purposes of God shall be accomplished, and the Great Jehovah shall say the work is done." (*History of the Church* 4:540.)

Great was the Prophet Joseph Smith's vision. It encompassed all the peoples of mankind, wherever they live, and all generations who have walked the earth and passed on. How can anyone, past or present, speak against him except out of ignorance? They have not tasted of his words; they have not pondered about him nor prayed about him. As one who has done these things, I add my own words of testimony that he was and is a prophet of God, raised up as an instrument in the hands of the Almighty to usher in a new and final gospel dispensation.

Of the Prophet we could say: "When a man gives his life for the cause he has advocated, he meets the highest test of his honesty and sincerity that his own or any future generation can in fairness ask. When he dies for the testimony he has borne, all malicious tongues should ever after be silent, and all voices hushed in reverence before a sacrifice so complete." (Ezra Dalby, *Ms.,* December 12, 1926.)

It is most fitting that today we sing in tribute to Joseph Smith, the great latter-day servant of our Lord and Master Jesus Christ:

100

Great is his glory and endless his priesthood.
Ever and ever the keys he will hold.
Faithful and true, he will enter his kingdom,
Crowned in the midst of the prophets of old.
    —*Hymns*, 1985, no. 27

CHAPTER 15

THE FAITH
OF THE PIONEERS

The tremendous progress of the Church in which all Latter-day Saints share is but the lengthened shadow of the faith and sacrifices of the devoted early Saints, the pioneers. It is good to look to the past to gain appreciation for the present and perspective for the future. It is good to look upon the virtues of those who have gone before, to gain strength for whatever lies ahead. It is good to reflect upon the work of those who labored so hard and gained so little in this world, but out of whose dreams and early plans, so well nurtured, has come a great harvest of which we are the beneficiaries. Their tremendous example can become a compelling motivation for us all, for each of us is a pioneer in his own life, often in his own family, and many pioneer daily in trying to establish a gospel foothold in distant parts of the world.

Can a generation that lives with central heating and air conditioning, with the automobile and the airplane, with the miracle of television and the magic of the computer, understand, appreciate, and learn from the lives and motives of those who had none of these and yet accomplished much of tremendous consequence?

In the environment in which many of us live, there is need for reminders of lessons learned in the past. In our times of abundance, it is good occasionally to be taken back to earlier days, to have our minds refocused on the struggles of the early Latter-day Saints, to remind us of the necessity for labor if the earth is to be made to yield, of the importance of faith in God if there is to be lasting achievement, and of the need to recognize that many of the so-called old values are worthy of present application.

Oh, how much is faith needed in each of our lives — faith in ourselves, faith in our associates, and faith in the living God.

Those pioneers who broke the sunbaked soil of the Mountain West came for one reason only: "to find," as Brigham Young is reported to have said, "a place where the devil can't come and dig us out." They found it, and against almost overwhelming adversities they subdued it. They cultivated and beautified it for themselves. And with inspired vision they planned and built a foundation that blesses members throughout the world today.

May I review some aspects of the faith of our early pioneers, a faith that carries tremendous impact for all of us — faith in self, faith in our associates, and faith in God.

FAITH IN SELF

On July 24, 1847, the pioneers entered Salt Lake Valley. They had traveled from the Missouri River, taking three months to cover the distance we cover in two hours by airplane. With faith in their capacity to do what needed doing, they set to work. Theirs was a philosophy of self-reliance. There was no government to assist them. They had natural resources, it is true. But they had to dig them out and fashion them. Their workmanship is a miracle to me. They had little more than their bare hands. Their tools were simple and relatively crude in comparison with ours. Of machinery they had little, and for the most part it was self-improvised. But they had skills, patiently learned, in masonry, the working of wood, the making and application of plaster, the setting of glass. The quality of their craftsmanship is not excelled in our time. In

103

many respects, it is not equaled. Those who look upon it today are quick to agree that it was inspired.

Many years ago I had a remarkable teacher at the University of Utah, a Jewish scholar, the first Jew to teach at a university in the state of Utah. He was from the East and came west with trepidation. As he walked up Main Street in Salt Lake City, his eye caught sight of the temple with the gold figure atop the highest tower. That temple was a thing of beauty and wonder to him. He spoke in years that followed of standing and looking at the temple, at the beauty of its symmetry, at the upward reach of its towers, at the strength of its design, at the remarkable detail of its workmanship. During all of the years that he lived in Salt Lake City it never became commonplace to him.

I walked through that temple recently. There was renewed in my mind a tremendous appreciation for its remarkable beauty and for the capacity of its builders.

Each year tourists from around the world visit the Salt Lake Tabernacle. They marvel at that magnificent and unique building, which was constructed more than a century ago in a spirit of self-reliance by a people who had faith that they could do great and remarkable things, notwithstanding serious handicaps, if they put their minds to doing them.

In that spirit of self-reliance they believed in education to qualify their children for responsibilities in the society of which they would become a part. Their library resources were extremely limited, but there was no limit on the inspiration of their teachers. Read the letters, the writings, the journals of those early pioneers who were the products of the simple schools of the day. They may have had some problems with capitalization and punctuation, but their powers of expression were tremendous. Their textbooks were few. They had the McGuffey readers, those remarkable books put together by William Holmes McGuffey beginning in 1836. The McGuffey reader used works by Shakespeare, Thoreau, Tennyson, and others of similar stature. Added to the wonderful language of these master writers, those simple textbooks unapologetically taught lessons on honesty, fairness, morality, and the work ethic.

FAITH IN OTHERS

Our pioneer forebears worked together for the common good. I am profoundly grateful for the essence of that spirit of helpfulness which has come down through the generations and which has been so evident in the troubles Latter-day Saints experience in time of disaster and difficulty. The mayor of Salt Lake City told me that when the Salt Lake City flood situation became serious one Sunday afternoon in 1983, he called a stake president, and within a very short time four thousand volunteers showed up. The story of such mutual helpfulness caught the attention of many individuals and publications across the nation. Latter-day Saints, working together with their neighbors of other faiths, have labored with one another in times of distress and have been heralded on radio and television, in newspapers and magazines. Writers have treated this as if it were a new and unique phenomenon. It is not new, although it may be unique in this time. I read with interest the comment of a federal relief official who said that those sent to Utah after the floods to offer government aid had received far fewer calls than they had anticipated. The fact is that many people simply said resolutely, as their forebears before them might have said, "We will work together and do what we need to do to restore our homes and farms." May God bless all who work unitedly with such faith and love and appreciation one for another in times of difficulty.

FAITH IN GOD

The pioneers regarded their move to the West as a blessing divinely given. Said Brigham Young on one occasion: "I do not wish men to understand I had anything to do with our being moved here, that was the providence of the Almighty; it was the power of God that wrought out salvation for this people, I never could have devised such a plan." (*Discourses of Brigham Young*, p. 480.)

The power that moved our gospel forebears was the power of faith in God. It was the same power that made possible the exodus from Egypt, the passage through the Red Sea, the long journey through the wilderness, and the establishment of Israel in the Promised Land.

It was by this power that our gospel forebears left Nauvoo and the beautiful lands of the Mississippi to travel to the shores of the Great Salt Lake. To me, it is a thing of never-ending wonder that Brigham Young and his associates had the faith to move to the mountain valleys of Utah. Of course, there were others who traversed the continent, but for the most part they were small groups. The movement of our people involved an exodus of many thousands to a land that others thought barren and unproductive. Nevertheless, they went west, putting their trust in God that he would rebuke the sterility of the soil and temper the climate so that they might be sustained and grow and become a mighty people in the midst of the Rocky Mountains in order to send from its bastions the word of truth everywhere. It was by the power of faith that they threaded their way up the Elkhorn and along the Platte, past Chimney Rock, and on to South Pass, down the Sweetwater to Independence Rock, and finally over Big Mountain and into the Salt Lake Valley.

I have often read the words of a thirteen-year-old girl, my wife's grandmother, Mary Goble Pay. I regard them as something of a classic. Her family was converted in Brighton, England, in 1856. They sold their possessions and sailed from Liverpool with nine hundred others on the vessel *Horizon*. After six weeks at sea, they landed at Boston. From there they traveled by steam train to Iowa City for fitting out, purchasing two yoke of oxen, one yoke of cows, a wagon, and a tent. They were assigned to travel with and assist one of the handcart companies.

At Iowa City their first tragedy also occurred. Their youngest child, less than two years of age and suffering from exposure, died and was buried in a grave never again visited by a member of the family. Mary Goble, then a thirteen-year-old girl, wrote of their experiences:

"We traveled from fifteen to twenty-five miles a day . . . till we got to the Platte River. . . . We caught up with the handcart companies that day. We watched them cross the river. There were great lumps of ice floating down the river. It was bitter cold. The next morning there were fourteen dead. . . . We went back to camp and had our prayers and . . . sang 'Come, Come Ye Saints, No Toil nor Labor Fear.' I wondered what made my mother cry that night. . . . The next morning my little sister was born. It was the twenty-third of September. We named her Edith. She lived six weeks and died. . . . She was buried at the last crossing of the Sweetwater.

"When we arrived at Devil's Gate it was bitter cold. We left many of our things there. . . . My brother James . . . was as well as he ever was when we went to bed that night. In the morning he was dead. . . . "

"My feet were frozen; also my brother's and my sister's. It was nothing but snow. We could not drive the pegs in our tents. . . . We did not know what would become of us. . . . Brigham Young had sent men and teams to help us. . . . We sang songs; some danced, and some cried. . . .

"My mother never got well. . . . She died between the Little and Big Mountains. . . . She was forty-three years of age. . . . We arrived in Salt Lake City nine o'clock at night the eleventh of December, 1856. Three out of the four that were living were frozen. My mother was dead in the wagon. . . .

"Early next morning Brigham Young came. . . . When he saw our condition, our feet frozen and our mother dead, tears rolled down his cheeks. . . . The doctor amputated my toes . . . while the sisters were dressing mother for her grave. . . . That afternoon she was buried.

"I have often thought of my mother's words before we left England. 'Polly, I want to go to Zion while my children

107

are small so that they can be raised in the Gospel of Jesus Christ.' "

This story is representative of the stories of thousands. It is an expression of a marvelous but simple faith, an unquestioning conviction, that the God of heaven in his power will make all things right and bring to pass his eternal purposes in the lives of his children. We need so very, very much a strong burning of that faith in the living God and in his living, resurrected Son, for this was the great, moving faith of our gospel forebears. Theirs was a vision, transcendent and overriding all other considerations. When they went west, they were a thousand miles, a thousand tedious miles, from the nearest settlements to the east and eight hundred miles from those to the west. A personal and individual recognition of God their Eternal Father to whom they could look in faith was of the very essence of their strength. They believed in that great scriptural mandate: "Look to God and live." (Alma 37:47.) With faith they sought to do his will. With faith they read and accepted divine teaching. With faith they labored until they dropped, always with a conviction that there would be an accounting to him who was their Father and their God.

Brigham Young's words concerning his own death and burial are worth noting. After giving instructions concerning where he should be buried, he said, "There let my earthly house or tabernacle rest in peace, and have a good sleep, until the morning of the first resurrection; no crying, no mourning with anyone *as I have done my work faithfully and in good faith.*" (Cited in Preston Nibley, *Brigham Young: The Man and His Work* [Salt Lake City: Deseret Book, 1936], p. 537. Italics added.)

As we reflect on those who have gone before us, and as we consider our present labors for the good of ourselves and others, would that we all might say each day, "I am doing my work faithfully and in good faith."

Let us look again to the power of faith in ourselves, faith in our associates, and faith in God our Eternal Father. Let us prayerfully implement such faith in our lives.

CHAPTER 16

TAKING
THE GOSPEL
TO BRITAIN

The resurrected Lord had said to his beloved disciples: "Go ye into all the world, and preach the gospel to every creature." (Mark 16:15.) That was a tremendous charge given to a handful of men who had neither means nor standing before the world to carry out that encompassing mandate! They gave their lives in doing all that they could.

Then John the Revelator in vision "saw another angel fly in the midst of heaven, having the everlasting gospel to preach unto them that dwell on the earth, and to every nation, and kindred, and tongue, and people." (Revelation 14:6.)

In these latter days, as Joseph Smith concluded his translation of the Book of Mormon, he arrived at the statement that has become part of the title page and that sets forth the book's purpose: "to show unto the remnant of the House of Israel what great things the Lord hath done for their fathers; and that they may know the covenants of the Lord, that they are not cast off forever—and also to the convincing of the Jew and Gentile that Jesus is the Christ, the Eternal God, manifesting himself unto all nations." (Title Page of the Book of Mormon.)

In the revelation given November 1, 1831, that became section 1 of the Doctrine and Covenants, the Lord said: "Hearken ye people from afar; and ye that are upon the islands of the sea, listen together. For verily the voice of the Lord is unto all men, and there is none to escape; and there is no eye that shall not see, neither ear that shall not hear, neither heart that shall not be penetrated. . . .

"And the voice of warning shall be unto all people, by the mouths of my disciples, whom I have chosen in these last days. And they shall go forth and none shall stay them, for I the Lord have commanded them." (D&C 1:1-2, 4-5.)

This was a God-given mandate, a millennial mandate. It rested upon a handful of Latter-day Saints living in the farming communities of Kirtland, Ohio, and its environs in the 1830s. They had very little money. At tremendous sacrifice they had constructed a temple as "a house of prayer, a house of fasting, a house of faith, a house of learning, a house of glory, a house of order, a house of God." (D&C 109:8.) With the dedication of that sacred edifice, the power of the adversary began to move through Kirtland, manifesting itself in a spirit of reckless speculation that diverted the minds of many from the things of God to the things of mammon. The United States at that time was gripped by this spirit of speculation, which burst with catastrophic effects in the financial crash of 1837. In Kirtland, people turned against the Prophet Joseph Smith. There was bitterness, and there was greed. The Church was shaken, and a great sifting took place between the faithful and those whose eyes were set upon the things of the world. The problem was compounded by the fact that some members were in Ohio and others were in Missouri, separated by a distance of eight hundred miles and largely without communication.

Here were a people with a millennial vision and a responsibility that encompassed the entire world, but who were embroiled in difficulties sapping the very lifeblood of the Church.

It was in these distressing times, on Sunday, June 4, 1837, that the Prophet Joseph Smith went to Elder Heber C. Kimball of the Quorum of the Twelve, while Brother Kimball "was seated in front of the stand, above the sacrament table on the

110

Melchisedek side of the Temple in Kirtland, and whispering to [him], said, 'Brother Heber, the Spirit of the Lord has whispered to me: Let my servant Heber go to England and proclaim my Gospel, and open the door of salvation to that nation.' " (*History of the Church* 2:490.)

Imagine, if you will, one man who had very little goods of the world telling another who had practically nothing, having just returned from a mission, that he was to go across the sea to open the work there. Wasn't there enough to be done at home? less faithful might have asked. They were on the frontier of the nation, and the entire membership of the Church probably did not exceed fifteen thousand people.

But there was a vision in the hearts of these men. It was a millennial vision that the gospel was to be preached to every nation before the end should come. Some work had been done in Canada, but now they were speaking of crossing the sea to the British Isles. One can understand Elder Kimball's response. Feeling his weakness he said, "O, Lord, I am a man of stammering tongue, and altogether unfit for such a work; how can I go to preach in that land, which is so famed throughout Christendom for learning, knowledge and piety; the nursery of religion; and to a people whose intelligence is proverbial!" (Orson F. Whitney, *Life of Heber C. Kimball* [Salt Lake City: Bookcraft, 1945], p. 104.)

The call of Elder Kimball and his associates to go to Britain was a declaration by the Prophet of the great destiny of this restored work. As I have read of the condition of the Saints in Ohio and Missouri at that time, and of the smallness of their number, I have marveled at the breadth of their vision. From that time forth there has never been a dimming of that vision. Through the years that followed, regardless of drivings, persecution, poverty, oppression, and every other force the adversary could exercise against them, the work has grown and expanded across the earth. Much as has been done, the end has not yet come. We have done practically nothing in many areas of the world, but as the doors of the nations open,

111

messengers of truth will go forward in fulfillment of that great millennial vision which was opened in the dark days of Ohio and Missouri with the call of seven men to go to the British Isles.

Their response to that call was a magnificent expression of faith. Said Elder Kimball at the time, "The idea of such a mission was almost more than I could bear up under. I was almost ready to sink under the burden which was placed upon me. However, all these considerations did not deter me from the path of duty; the moment I understood the will of my Heavenly Father, I felt a determination to go at all hazards, believing that He would support me by His almighty power, and endow me with every qualification that I needed; and although my family was dear to me, and I should have to leave them almost destitute, I felt that the cause of truth, the Gospel of Christ, outweighed every other consideration." (Ibid., p. 104.)

Orson Hyde, Willard Richards, and Joseph Fielding responded with similar faith, and these four were joined in New York by John Goodson, Isaac Russell, and John Snyder, who came forward with comparable faith for that historic and significant undertaking.

Tuesday, June 13, was the scheduled departure date for the four who were to leave Kirtland. One who looked in on the Kimball household that morning described the prayer that was uttered by the father who was leaving and who then, "like the patriarchs, and by virtue of his office, laid his hands upon [the heads of his children] individually, leaving a father's blessing upon them, and commending them to the care and protection of God, while he should be engaged preaching the Gospel in a foreign land. While thus engaged his voice was almost lost in the sobs of those around, who tried in vain to suppress them. The idea of being separated from their protector and father for so long a time was indeed painful. He proceeded, but his heart was too much affected to do so regularly. His emotions were great, and he was obliged to stop at intervals, while the big tears rolled down his cheeks." (Ibid., pp. 108-9.)

Faith? Faith was all they had—faith and courage. They had no money. One of the brethren gave the coatless Heber a coat. One of the women gave him five dollars, with which he paid for passage for himself and Orson Hyde to Buffalo. En route to New York City they went by way of Massachusetts and collected forty dollars from a brother of Willard Richards.

They met their associates in New York, and on Sunday, June 25, they noted that they fasted, prayed, administered the sacrament, and pleaded with the Lord for direction. Somehow they secured eighteen dollars each for passage to Liverpool. At ten o'clock on the morning of July 1, they boarded the packet ship *Garrick,* which soon drew anchor, hoisted sails, and started across the sea.

What an expression of faith and what a demonstration of courage! That courage carried with it a spirit of enthusiasm. After eighteen days and eighteen hours on the water, to cover a distance I flew on a Concorde Super-Service jet in three hours and twenty minutes, the ship pulled into the Mersey River beside the dock at Liverpool, England. A small boat came alongside the larger ship. They boarded this, and when they were within six or seven feet of the shore, Heber jumped to shore. The missionaries spent a few days in Liverpool seeking direction from the Lord, and then they felt the confirming whispering of the Spirit directing them to go thirty-one miles north to the town of Preston. There they found a city in a state of excitement. Queen Victoria had ascended the throne three days earlier and had called for a national election for members of Parliament.

As the Mormon missionaries walked up the street in Preston, a banner unfurled before them bearing the words "Truth Will Prevail." This they adopted as the motto of their mission. Their work immediately became a declaration of everlasting truth. They preached first in Vauxhall Chapel, whose minister was a brother of Joseph Fielding of their own group. That

113

and their subsequent preachings led to the baptism of nine souls in the River Ribble the following Sunday.

From that July day in 1837 their message of truth has been repeated by thousands of missionaries who have followed them, and it has come to lodge in the hearts of hundreds of thousands who have accepted the gospel in the British Isles.

I am one of those missionaries who followed them. My sacrifice was not as great. I fear my faith was not as strong. Certainly my journey was not as tedious as was theirs. I traveled by train in 1933 from Salt Lake City to New York and then took a ship to Plymouth, England. There were three of us in our group. Two stayed in London, and somehow, in the providence of the Lord, I, like Heber C. Kimball and his associates ninety-six years earlier, was sent to Preston.

That was my first assignment and my first field of labor. I became as familiar with the places they knew and the streets they walked as they had been nearly a century earlier. My companion and I walked up and down the same road where they had seen that banner with the motto "Truth Will Prevail."

In the evening of the first day that I arrived in Preston, my companion, who was the district president, said we would go down to the marketplace and hold a street meeting. There, in the public square that had been familiar to Heber C. Kimball and his associates, Elder Bramwell and I raised our voices in a hymn, offered prayer, and preached the same gospel to a gathering crowd just as those first missionaries had preached.

The location of the house in Wilfred Street where they stayed and had a terrible experience with evil spirits, was also familiar to me. Years later, I took President Spencer W. Kimball there so that he might see where his grandfather had that terrifying experience.

Each missionary day as my companion and I walked along Manchester Road to and from our "digs," we passed Vauxhall Chapel again and again, as did those first missionaries when they preached within its walls the day after they arrived in Preston. I was there some years later when a bulldozer was knocking the old building down to make way for a housing project. I picked up a brick from that chapel, which I still have. The River Ribble with its old tram bridge, where the first baptisms were performed while hundreds of people looked on, was also familiar to me.

I feel especially fortunate to have been sent to Preston as my initial assignment. Not only did I labor there, but I labored in the surrounding towns where those first missionaries taught the gospel. I was not as effective as were they. When they first arrived, there evidently was little or no prejudice against them. When I arrived, it seemed that everyone was prejudiced against us.

I was not well when I arrived. Those first few weeks, because of illness and the opposition we felt, I was discouraged. I wrote a letter home to my good father and said that I felt I was wasting my time and his money. He was my father and my stake president, and he was a wise and inspired man. He wrote a very short letter to me and said, "Dear Gordon, I have your recent letter. I have only one suggestion: forget yourself and go to work." Earlier that morning in our scripture class my companion and I had read these words of the Lord: "Whosoever will save his life shall lose it; but whosoever shall lose his life for my sake and the gospel's, the same shall save it." (Mark 8:35.)

Those words of the Master, followed by my father's letter with his counsel to forget myself and go to work, went into my very being. With my father's letter in hand, I went into our bedroom in the house at 15 Wadham Road, where we lived, and got on my knees and made a pledge with the Lord. I covenanted that I would try to forget myself and lose myself in his service.

That July day in 1933 was my day of decision. A new light came into my life and a new joy into my heart. The fog of England seemed to lift, and I saw the sunlight. I had a rich and wonderful mission experience, for which I shall ever be grateful, laboring in Preston where the work began and in

115

other places where it had moved forward, including the great city of London, where I served the larger part of my mission.

I feel thankful for the events of 1837, for the call by the Prophet Joseph Smith to those early missionaries to go to Britain in declaration of a great millennial vision, in expression of a tremendous faith, in demonstration of personal courage, with a statement of everlasting truth. I am profoundly grateful that while laboring on the ground they hallowed by their efforts, there came into my heart a consuming love for the work of God and for his Beloved Son, the Redeemer of the world, in whose name we serve as members of his church.

God be thanked for the glorious gospel, restored to earth in this the "dispensation of the fulness of times."

God be thanked for the Prophet Joseph Smith, through whom that restoration came, and for the revelation given and received only seven years after the founding of the Church to take the gospel to the isles of Britain.

God be thanked for the faith of those who, with neither purse nor scrip, sailed the ocean and began the work that has gone forward without interruption now for more than a century and a half. From there the work spread to Europe, and now to much of the world.

The infusion of the blood of Britain into the weakened body of the Church in 1837 and in the years that followed gave much needed strength. From those isles came thousands of converts, many with skills that became useful in building Nauvoo and, later, the communities of the western valleys. I never look upon the magnificent Salt Lake Temple and Tabernacle, the other temples in Utah, the Lion and Beehive houses, and various other Church structures they built without marveling at their handiwork. Hundreds died on the journey to the mountain valleys. But they and those who lived to settle there left a residual of faith in harmony with that which was carried by the small group who in 1837 cast the gospel net in England.

May we remember that each of us has the privilege and opportunity, by the manner of our lives and the power of our witness, to make our own declaration of faith, courage, and truth that will help bring to fulfillment the God-given mandate to take the gospel to the world.

CHAPTER 17

GO
FORWARD
WITH FAITH

Some time ago I was in Kirtland, Ohio, with President Ezra Taft Benson to dedicate the Newell K. Whitney store, which has been restored by the Church. As nearly as the architects and historians can determine, the building has been restored to the condition it was in when Joseph Smith first entered it. On or about February 1, 1831, he stepped from the sleigh in which he had traveled from New York to Kirtland, opened the front door, stepped to one of the proprietors at the counter, and said, "Newell K. Whitney. Thou art the man."

Newell Whitney was surprised until the Prophet introduced himself and said that Newell had prayed him there. Thus commenced a long and trusted association that changed the life and career of Newell K. Whitney and set in motion events that shaped the history of the Church.

The Whitney store was presumably a regular commercial establishment in the village of Kirtland. Calico and ribbons, hardware and cooking utensils, and a host of other items were sold as a part of a thriving business in a rather vigorous community. But every rural community of any consequence had such a general store, so why was this one so special?

One reason the Church has gone to great effort to restore the building is that Joseph and Emma Smith lived there for some time. That is significant, but more significant is the fact that the School of the Prophets (sometimes called the School of the Elders) was held there. It was a gathering place of the leading brethren of the day. It was designed and conducted as a place of training, principally for missionary service. This was a time of outpouring of knowledge from the heavens, when many revelations were received as the foundations of this great work were being laid.

I commented when I was there that if New York represented the birthplace of the Church, then Ohio represented the period of schooling for the young prophet and his associates. It was a time when the Church was operating in two spheres—Ohio and Missouri—eight hundred miles apart. Transportation was most tedious and difficult. There was, of course, no telegraph or other means of easy communication. It was a time when there was much bitterness and persecution. It was a time when there was much apostasy and many vile accusations.

But it was also a marvelous and miraculous season, a time of pentecostal outpouring. Sixty-two of the revelations found in the Doctrine and Covenants were received during that Ohio period and in that environment. During that time, the Kirtland Temple was constructed and there occurred many miraculous events incident to its dedication. Moses, Elias, and Elijah came, bestowing eternal priesthood keys. The Son of God appeared to his servants, and they bore testimony of him. The work was strengthened and integrated in a most remarkable manner.

Of that season Orson Pratt said, "God was there, his angels were there, the Holy Ghost was in the midst of the people, the visions of the Almighty were opened to the minds of the servants of the living God; the veil was taken from the minds of many; they saw the heavens opened; they beheld the angels of God; they heard the voice of the Lord; and they were filled from the crown of their heads to the soles of their feet with the power and inspiration of the Holy Ghost." (*Journal of Discourses* 18:132.)

This was also the season—those seven years between 1831

and 1838—of harsh and unrelenting persecution. Enemies threatened to knock down the walls of the temple. Philastus Hurlburt was excommunicated and in bitterness set in motion the Spaulding manuscript story of the origin of the Book of Mormon, with all of the mischief that for years followed that concoction. The Kirtland bank failed. The Prophet and Sidney Rigdon were taken from their homes, dragged through the cold of a March night, tarred and feathered, and left for dead. In addition to all of this, troubles equally as serious were being experienced in Missouri, the other center of the Church.

I have frequently reflected on how Joseph Smith must have felt at those times. He was directly or indirectly responsible for all of the misery and suffering that occurred. Did doubt occasionally assail his mind? I find the exact opposite in the revelations that came through him during that period. While sitting in the John Johnson home in Hiram, Ohio, I reflected on the words of section 1 of the Doctrine and Covenants, which was given as a revelation at Hiram on November 1, 1831, as a preface to the forthcoming publication of "the doctrines, covenants, and commandments given in this dispensation"—what has now become our Doctrine and Covenants.

We need to get a picture in our minds of the setting. Here was the leader of a little group of people in Ohio, numbering at the time perhaps three hundred, scattered through frontier communities where there was much bitterness and hatred. But with vision both prophetic and bold he declared in the name of the Lord: "Verily the voice of the Lord is unto all men, and there is none to escape; and there is no eye that shall not see, neither ear that shall not hear, neither heart that shall not be penetrated. And the rebellious shall be pierced with much sorrow. . . . And the voice of warning shall be unto all people, by the mouths of my disciples, whom I have chosen in these last days. And they shall go forth and none shall stay them, for I the Lord have commanded them." (D&C 1:2-5.)

120

Later in that same revelation were set forth the grand objectives of this great latter-day work:

1. "That every man might speak in the name of God the Lord, even the Savior of the world."

2. "That faith also might increase in the earth."

3. "That mine everlasting covenant might be established."

4. "That the fulness of my gospel might be proclaimed by the weak and the simple unto the ends of the world, and before kings and rulers . . . that they might come to understanding." (See D&C 1:20-24.)

These are truly remarkable objectives. It was not a country pastor who spoke these words. It was a prophet of the living God setting forth the depth and breadth and length of this great restored kingdom that was to go over the earth. In that remarkable revelation, the truth of the Book of Mormon was declared and the validity of the revelations was affirmed. Bold as were these declarations, there was no apology. Said the Lord, without equivocation: "What I the Lord have spoken, I have spoken, and I excuse not myself; and though the heavens and the earth pass away, my word shall not pass away, but shall all be fulfilled, whether by mine own voice or by the voice of my servants, it is the same." (D&C 1:38.)

Some time ago I noted the publication of a book put together by unbelievers as a "history" of the Church. I have not read the book, but the conclusion, reported one reviewer, is that the future of the Church is dim. Without wishing to seem impertinent, I should like to ask what the authors know about that future. They know nothing of the prophetic mission of the Church! The future must have looked extremely dim in the 1830s. It must have looked impossible back in those Ohio-Missouri days. But notwithstanding murders, notwithstanding confiscation and drivings and disfranchisement forced upon the Saints in the ensuing years, the work moved steadily on. It has continued to go forward. Never before has it been so strong. Never before has it been so widespread. Never before have there been so many in whose hearts has burned an unquenchable knowledge of the truth.

It is the work of the Almighty. It is the work of his Beloved Son, the Lord Jesus Christ. It is the gospel of salvation. Men and women may oppose now, just as others opposed in those days, but the work goes on because it is true and it is divine.

These are the best of times in the history of this work. What a wonderful privilege and great responsibility are ours to be an important part of this latter-day work of God. Do not become sidetracked by the wiles of Satan that seem so rampant in our era. Then as now we have critics. We even have those inside the Church who seem to delight in looking for every element of weakness in the past or the present.

Rather, let us go forward with faith and with the vision of the marvelous future that lies ahead as this work grows in strength and gains in momentum. Let us build faith in the hearts of all those around us.

In Kirtland, a school of the prophets was established to teach those young in the faith. In our homes and Church activities, we now teach in the schools of the future prophets. In all these settings, let us teach with power and conviction and faith. Let there always be an affirmation of testimony in the work of which we a part. And let us not forget these words of revelation, also given at Hiram, Ohio: "The keys of the kingdom of God are committed unto man on the earth, and from thence shall the gospel roll forth unto the ends of the earth, as the stone which is cut out of the mountain without hands shall roll forth, until it has filled the whole earth." (D&C 65:2.)

May the Lord bless us as builders of faith. May our testimonies strengthen and become as anchors to which others may secure their faith in hours of doubt and concern. May the candle of learning ever burn in our minds. Above all, may testimony grow in our hearts that this is in reality the church of the living God and that it will continue to move forward to fulfill its divine destiny. May we each do our part faithfully and with thanksgiving to the Lord for all the blessings he so wondrously bestows upon us as we follow his teachings and draw near to him.

SOURCES

The chapters in this book have been adapted from the following:

Chapter 1, "Faith, the Essence of True Religion": *Ensign,* October 1981, pp. 5-8.

Chapter 2, "The Cornerstone of Our Faith": *Ensign,* November 1984, pp. 50-53.

Chapter 3, "God Hath Not Given Us the Spirit of Fear": *Ensign,* October 1984, pp. 2-5.

Chapter 4, "The Father, the Son, and the Holy Ghost": *Ensign,* November 1986, pp. 49-51.

Chapter 5, "The Healing Power of Christ": *Ensign,* October 1988, pp. 52-54, 59.

Chapter 6, "Whosoever Will Save His Life": *Ensign,* August 1982, pp. 3-6.

Chapter 7, "And the Greatest of These Is Love": *Ensign,* March 1984, pp. 3-5.

Chapter 8, "We Have a Work to Do": *Ensign,* February 1988, pp. 2-6.

Chapter 9, "Building Faith through the Book of Mormon": *Ensign,* June 1988, pp. 2-6.

Chapter 10, "The Environment of Our Homes": *Ensign,* June 1985, pp. 3-6.

Chapter 11, "The Continuing Pursuit of Truth": *Ensign,* April 1986, pp. 2-6.

Chapter 12, "With All Thy Getting Get Understanding": *Ensign,* August 1988, pp. 2-5.

Chapter 13, "Small Acts Lead to Great Consequences": *Ensign,* May 1984, pp. 81-84.

Chapter 14, "Praise to the Man": *Ensign,* August 1983, pp. 2-6.

Chapter 15, "The Faith of the Pioneers": *Ensign,* July 1984, pp. 3-6.

Chapter 16, "Taking the Gospel to Great Britain": *Ensign,* July 1987, pp. 2-7.

Chapter 17, "Go Forward with Faith": *Ensign,* August 1986, pp. 3-5.

INDEX